How to Play
UKULELE

A Complete Guide for Beginners

DAN "COOL HAND UKE" SCANLAN

ADAMS MEDIA

NEW YORK   LONDON   TORONTO   SYDNEY   NEW DELHI

Aadamsmedia

Adams Media
An Imprint of Simon & Schuster, Inc.
57 Littlefield Street
Avon, Massachusetts 02322

First Adams Media trade paperback edition June 2018

ADAMS MEDIA and colophon are trademarks of Simon & Schuster.

For information about special discounts for bulk purchases, please contact Simon & Schuster Special Sales at 1-866-506-1949 or business@simonandschuster.com.

The Simon & Schuster Speakers Bureau can bring authors to your live event. For more information or to book an event contact the Simon & Schuster Speakers Bureau at 1-866-248-3049 or visit our website at www.simonspeakers.com.

Interior design by Colleen Cunningham
Interior images by Eric Andrews

Manufactured in the United States of America

9 2021

Library of Congress Cataloging-in-Publication Data
Scanlan, Dan, author.
How to play ukulele / Dan "Cool Hand Uke" Scanlan.
Avon, Massachusetts: Adams Media, 2018.
Series: How to play.
Includes bibliographical references and index.
LCCN 2017059007 | ISBN 9781507207499 (pb) | ISBN 9781507207505 (ebook)
LCSH: Ukulele--Instruction and study.
LCC MT645 .S37 2018 | DDC 787.8/9193--dc23
LC record available at https://lccn.loc.gov/2017059007

ISBN 978-1-5072-0749-9
ISBN 978-1-5072-0750-5 (ebook)

This book is dedicated to those who seek peace through music.

CONTENTS

Chapter 6. Let's Play 91

Chapter 7. Keeping On 111

ACKNOWLEDGMENTS

I am deeply indebted to my editors Julia Jacques and Brianne Keith, who marshaled me through the unfamiliar throes of publication. A deep thank-you, too, to Fred Fallin, Chicago's keeper of ukulele lore, and ethnomusicologist Gisa Jaehnichen of Germany, who have given me so many insights into the historical significance of the ukulele. I am deeply appreciative of R. Bruce of Australia, Pat Sauer of Albuquerque, New Mexico, and the late Buddy Craig and his wife, Emmeline, for the use of their wonderful tunes in this project. Thanks to Beverly Marks and Dr. William Dubrow for their talent in committing original songs to sheet music. And a special hug to my wife, Joan Buffington, who supported me in the long days and nights on this project.

INTRODUCTION

Hooray for taking up the ukulele! It will never let you down. People of all ages make great music with it, and they reap huge rewards from this instrument with the sweet, happy voice and glorious past.

Many people are pleasantly surprised to learn that once they pick up the ukulele, they instantly become members of a thriving, worldwide community—folks who love the ukulele, regardless of skill level or how long they have been playing. This vast community of enthusiastic players cheerily share what they have learned and are eager to find something new to play: a song, perhaps, or strum, or technique. The quest to conquer a strumming or picking pattern, tune, or style never ends. Be ready to learn from others and rejoice when you unexpectedly find yourself teaching another player something you have mastered. (The more often you teach others, the better player you become.) It's all part of being a ukulele player, an instrument with a great history and treasure chest of lore.

Although there have been ukulele groups, clubs, and festivals since the turn of the last century, they have swelled in recent times and popped up all over the world. International ukulele festivals, meet-ups, jams, and ceilidhs (parties with music, dancing, and storytelling) bring people together from many countries in an exhilarating atmosphere.

The ukulele gives voice to every kind of music: rock and roll, folk, Dixieland, country western, blues, classical, bluegrass, sacred, and more. We'll take a gander at many of them and try some on for size and fit—and, of course, for the fun of it.

After a brief history and handy tour of the instrument itself, this book will give you a "bump start" so you can begin playing the ukulele right away.

The book follows the three basic elements of music: rhythm, harmony, and melody. **Rhythm** is that part of music that you dance or tap your toe to. So much of playing the ukulele is in the strums you choose. We'll explore a variety of them, and other rhythm techniques, using familiar tunes. You don't want to miss this chapter.

Harmony is two or more notes played together that please the ear. Most often three notes are used in what is called a chord. Chords change during a song and form a kind of architecture or skeleton of the song. Chords enrich our songs with emotion and, sometimes, suspense and resolution. This is a chapter you will want to visit often and consider to be a space where growth never ends. Some chords may seem at first as if you will never be able to play them. But you can. I'll show you how.

Melody is that part of a song you can whistle, hum, or sing. It consists of individual notes that rise and fall and have long or short durations. It's the part of a song we are quickest to recognize. To capture the idea of melody, we will explore a variety of scales—note sequences. It will be fun.

Doo-dads are things you can goof around with on the ukulele that don't easily fall into any of the previously listed categories. They tend to be fun and can give your playing personality. Good to know.

Songs are what happens when you play music. This chapter will feature a few easy-to-play songs, a few that are a little more challenging, and a couple of what I like to call "stretch out" tunes: tunes that you might want to take a year or two to get into your DNA. I started working on Hoagy Carmichael's "Stardust" in 1961 and didn't really feel as if I owned it until about 1990. Truly a "stretch out" song. The more you work on the hard songs, the more other songs become a piece of cake to learn.

Keeping On is about practicing and learning and, well, keeping on track while gathering your ukulele skills. A small repository of practical advice.

Reference (Chapter 8 and Appendix A) includes a glossary of ukulele and music terminology, some useful chord charts, substitutions, and an explanation of the Circle of Fifths. Hopefully, it'll be a handy place to peek at once in a while.

Resources provides links to ukulele clubs, groups, festivals, players, songs, and videos. I hope they don't tie you up on the Internet so much that you don't have time to play your ukulele!

Okay, now let's get ukin'.

—Dan "Cool Hand Uke" Scanlan

Chapter 1

GETTING TO KNOW

YOUR UKULELE

In this chapter, you'll get to know your ukulele—where it came from, what each part does, and general advice on how to hold it and take care of it so you can keep your ukulele healthy and in good shape. Let's begin the tour.

Who Invented the Ukulele?

The ukulele was invented in 1879 when three enterprising woodworkers from Madeira Island, a Portuguese island off the coast of North Africa, arrived in Hawaii looking for business with their fellow countrymen already living there. Well, business wasn't looking good, and Manuel Nunes and his friends Augusto Dias and José do Espirito Santo knew they needed to get creative to survive.

When the three arrived in Hawaii on the ship SS *Ravenscrag* with some 300 other Madeirans, fellow passenger João Fernandes danced down the gangplank playing a braguinha, a small four-string Madeiran folk instrument. This high-pitched, energetically played instrument tickled the Hawaiians. That's when Nunes, Dias, and Santo realized they might be onto something: could they make a living by combining two popular folk instruments of their island—the rajão and the braguinha?

The rajão was a five-string Madeiran folk instrument, smaller than a guitar but using similar fingering formations. It had no bass string, but it did have re-entrant tuning (to be discussed later in this chapter). The strings were tuned DGCEA with the D and G strings tuned a whole octave higher than one would expect. The men took the four strings from the rajão (the GCE and A) and placed them on the smaller braguinha. (In effect, the ukulele took its size from the braguinha and its tuning from the rajão.) They called their new invention the "mini rajão."

When they were finished, the trio wisely took their mini rajão to King David Kalakaua, the last monarch of Hawaii, who was a guitar player. The king could instantly play it and loved it. Soon the Hawaiian people fell in love with it as well. It's safe to say that in 1879, the rajão and the braguinha went to Hawaii, married, and gave birth to the ukulele.

By 1900, the ukulele had firmly earned its place in Hawaiian history. It became Hawaii's favorite souvenir (some historians assert the ukulele was the world's first official souvenir of any nation), and Hawaiian bands featuring the ukulele began touring the United States.

Ukulele Parts

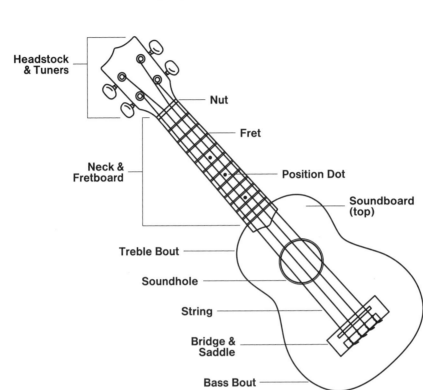

Headstock & Tuners

Nut

Fret

Neck & Fretboard

Position Dot

Soundboard (top)

Treble Bout

Soundhole

String

Bridge & Saddle

Bass Bout

UKE TIP

So, what about the strange name? *Ukulele* is most likely a pun based on *lele*, meaning "to jump," and *ukeke*, a one-string mouth harp indigenous to Hawaii. Because of the energetic way it is played, *ukulele* is often translated as "jumping flea," a concept that led to the familiar mnemonic "my dog has fleas," which is used for tuning. King Kalakaua's sister, Princess Lili'uokalani, who also quickly took to the instrument (and whose song "Aloha 'Oe" became one of the first tunes associated with it), preferred the translation "the gift that came here."

Head and Neck

We'll begin with the head and neck. The headstock, or head, is the top part of the neck. It is where you will find the tuners. Tuners, also called machine heads, pegheads, or tuning machines, are the objects protruding from the headstock and are tightened or loosened to manipulate the sound of the strings. Tuners on the earliest ukuleles were like the wooden ones on violins. Today you'll find they're usually made of steel. Peghead tuners are a modern 4:1-geared tuner (that is, four turns of the paddle rotates the peg one time). Most tuners loosen over time with use. They can usually be tightened by turning a small screw at the end of the paddle.

How to hold your uke.

On the back of the instrument, where the head meets the neck, is the heel. The heel is important to the player—it must feel good (and to the luthier, or maker, look good), properly secure the neck to the body, and withstand the strain of stretched strings being energetically strummed.

On the front of the instrument, where the head meets the neck, you'll find the nut. Its job is to keep the strings in place. Nuts can be made of all sorts of materials—metal, bone, ebony, plastic, or composite materials—and have slots cut into them where the strings are nestled. Slots are cut so they follow the angle of the head. When a slot is cut too low, it can cause the string to buzz or be deadened at the first fret. When a slot is cut too high, it can cause the string to go sharp at the first fret. It can also be painful to play, and that's not good—nothing should discourage a player from playing. Generally speaking, a credit card should slide easily but snugly between the string and the first fret.

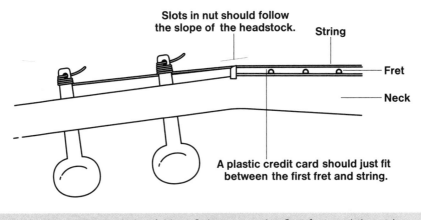

Slots in nut should follow the slope of the headstock.

String

Fret

Neck

A plastic credit card should just fit between the first fret and string.

A plastic credit card should just fit between the first fret and the string.

The nut is considered zero fret (some guitar makers put a zero fret in front of the nut to mark it). It marks one end of the "open" (unfretted) strings. It's crucial that the strings are held in place; otherwise the string would move around a lot and result in a sound you might not want.

The neck connects the head and body. Necks can be reinforced with materials like ebony or carbon fiber rods. Along the neck runs the fretboard and position dots. Along the fretboard run wires from nut to bridge that follow an ascending chromatic scale. Each fret represents one half step. For example, the open A string becomes A♯ or B♭ when the space between the nut and the first fret is depressed. The next fret gives a B, the next C, the next C♯, and so on.

♫

UKE TIP

After years of use, a re-fret job will make some instruments play much better. A luthier will remove each fret and insert and glue a new one. When a fret becomes loose in its slot, it will cause dull tones. When replacing strings, it is a good idea to "dress" the entire fretboard lightly with a few swipes of fine sandpaper, steel wool, or a ScotchBrite pad.

Position dots, or fretmarkers, tell players where they are as they play. They are usually placed at the fifth, seventh, tenth, and twelfth frets along the fretboard, sometimes even higher. Some instruments have dots that face the player. Dots are painted, inlaid, or made of symbols. See the illustration for properly fingering a fret.

The head, heel, and neck are usually made of one solid piece of wood. Maple, koa, or mahogany are some of the more common types of wood used. In more expensive versions luthiers may use several laminations of wood. In older ukuleles, slots are cut into the actual neck to hold the frets.

Strings

The strings are one of your major sound-making elements of the ukulele. Ukulele strings are usually made of nylon or plastic. Sometimes the C string is wound, meaning one string is wrapped in another. This creates a mellower low middle C note, but at a lower volume. Usually a string is attached at one end by a large knot secured in a hole and groove in the bridge, and at the other end by winding it around the tuning peg several times. It is then threaded once or twice through the hole in the peg. Some bridges require the string to pass through a hole at the back of the bridge, then cross over the bridge and wrap around itself. See the illustration for both methods.

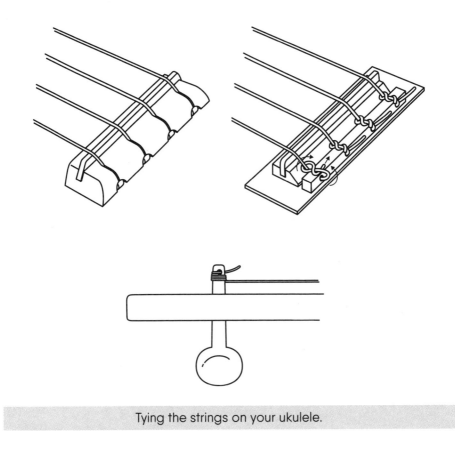

Tying the strings on your ukulele.

The Main Body

The body can be thought of as having two main parts—the treble bout and the bass bout, which are separated by the waist. The treble bout produces the high tones, and the bass bout gives deeper, lower tones. The original ukuleles built by Nunes, Santos, and Dias had very long waists and narrow bouts. Today, ukuleles are wider. The soundboard is usually a single piece of wood that makes up the top of the instrument.

In the middle of the body is the soundhole. Soundholes are usually round, sometimes oval. The purpose of the soundhole is to allow sound to pass and the body to reverberate. Some luthiers are now experimenting with the shapes of soundholes to create new sounds and distinguish their instruments from the others. Beneath the soundhole is the bridge and the saddle. The saddle is the slotted piece that rests on the bridge. Like the nut, the strings are held in place by the saddle at the opposite end.

Finally, we come to the bindings and rosettes. These are mostly ornamental features, but don't be fooled—they are actually functional. Bindings can help strengthen the edges of the body and sometimes the fretboard. Rosettes can help strengthen the soundhole. Bindings may or may not add to the sound of the instrument—it depends on who you talk to. In any case, they sure can look good and may help make the player want to play even more.

♫

UKE TIP

Ukulele strings usually need to be replaced after a year. They should also be replaced when they become dirty, when they develop little cuts, or when they just sound dull. It can take some time for new strings to "settle down." One trick is to tune the ukulele up a few steps higher, play the instrument energetically, and then tune it back to standard pitch.

Tuning Your Ukulele

The ukulele has re-entrant tuning. Re-entrant tuning means that instead of the strings going from low to high as on a piano or guitar, one of the strings (the G string, in the case of the ukulele) "re-enters the scale" from a different position in the musical scale. This re-entrant G string gives the ukulele the "my dog has fleas" sound, starting an octave higher than expected, then going low and working its way back up.

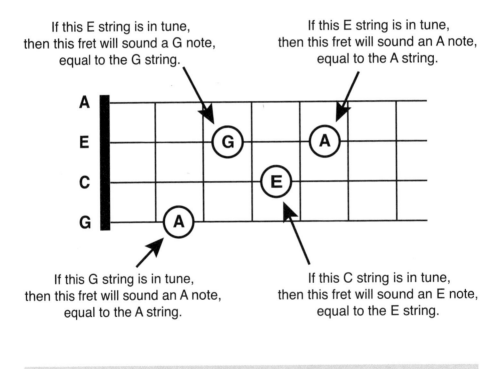

How to tune your ukulele.

There are several ways to tune a ukulele: by ear, to itself, or to an external device. If you are lucky enough to be among the few people who were blessed with perfect pitch, you can simply tune the strings to GCE and A, with the C being the middle C on the piano. The G string will be the same as the G on the third fret of the E string.

When I began playing ukulele in the early 1960s, I had a very poor sense of pitch. Because of the different "timbre" (distinctive sound that belongs to a specific instrument) of the sound of a blown pitch pipe and that of a plucked string, I had no confidence in what I was hearing. I learned to tune the ukulele by sight! When two strings are on the same pitch, the plucked string will cause the other one to vibrate. When I could make the G string jiggle when I played the G on the third fret of the E string, my confidence in the accuracy of my tuning increased. Check it out.

UKULELE HEROES

Roy and Kathy Sakuma produce the longest-running Annual Ukulele Festival in Honolulu. Roy's teaching efforts have kept the ukulele alive and well among the young people of Hawaii. Visit his website at http://roysakuma.net/.

Chapter 2

RHYTHM

Rhythm is the first element in music. We are born with rhythm—our heartbeat. For the ukulele, the **strum** is its "heartbeat," its rhythm. In this chapter, we'll explore a variety of strumming techniques and patterns that will set you up to play your first song. The goal is to master the ones covered here so they become part of your own personal "ukulele player's toolbox"—the bank of techniques and strumming patterns that will become the bedrock of your unique playing style.

Different strums are like colors on a palette, chosen and mixed by the artist to express different feelings. There are no right or wrong strums, but they all should be stumble-free and have a smooth sense of time. Revisit this chapter from time to time to remind yourself how far you've come and to discover what may be further possible. You might even find yourself inventing your own new strums after a first read.

♫

UKE TIP

Read this chapter with a ukulele in your hand. Make sure it is in tune. We not only learn strums here; we also train our ears.

The One-Finger Chord

Before we work on rhythm, we need to get a chord under our belt. A chord is a group of notes that are played together and is the building block of music, the distinctive sound you want to produce with your ukulele. (There'll be more on chords in Chapter 3.) Because we want to focus on strumming first, let's start with an easy chord. How easy? Well, you'll only need one finger to play it.

Here is a drawing of the C chord, a one-finger chord. For the C chord, you'll use the ring finger (3 dot) of your left hand. The dot shows that you should place that finger on the third fret of the first string, the A string.

When you play a chord, you shorten the length of one or more strings by holding it down. This is called **fretting**, and it is the action you take to create the sound. When you first play a chord, you might find that the sound has a rattle or buzz or just sounds dull. This is to be expected. You'll need to take the time to find the best angle to position your fingers to avoid this and create the clearest tone. See the following diagram for how to fret properly.

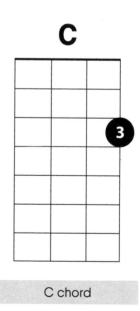

C chord

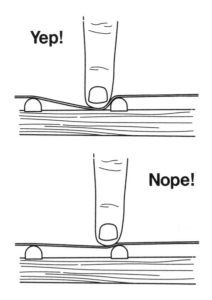

This is how you want to position your fingers
to get the clearest, cleanest sound.

UKE TIP

As you remember from the tuning section in Chapter 1, this book uses GCEA tuning. So as you look at this diagram (and those in the rest of this book), the strings should be read as **G**, **C**, **E**, and **A**, from left to right. The top horizontal line represents the **nut**, and the other horizontal lines represent the **frets**. Your fingers will be represented as numbered dots as follows:

- 1 = index finger
- 2 = middle finger

- 3 = ring finger
- 4 = pinkie finger

The dot shows you where to place the finger.

UKE TIP

When ukulele performer and radio personality May Singhi Breen convinced music publishers to include ukulele chord diagrams in sheet music during the 1920s, she helped establish the ukulele as a standard instrument and cement its popularity in the United States. Many publishers continue this practice today.

To get a clear tone, you'll want to press the string down *behind* the fret, not *on top* of it. This is important. To explore just how important, move your finger around to discover how disconcerting a misplaced finger can sound. Doesn't sound too good, right?

It's also important that you *avoid touching the other strings* when you play chords, especially one-finger chords. A little practice and attention will go a long way here, so keep at it. Your goal is that clear, clean sound.

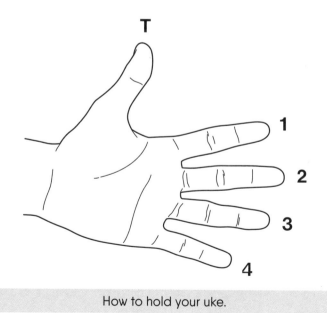

How to hold your uke.

Lastly, let's make sure you're holding your ukulele properly. If you are sitting, rest the body of the ukulele on your right leg and hold the other end by resting the neck in the valley between the thumb and index finger of your left hand. If you prefer to stand, pinch the body of the ukulele between your right forearm and right side of your belly. Now place your left ring finger in the space behind the third fret of the A string (the one closest to the ground). You're now ready to play the one-finger C chord.

Start with a Strum

With a relaxed up-and-down movement, drag your right index finger across the strings, striking them near the spot where the neck meets the body. Use both up-and-down movements on your arm and swivel your wrist.

Easy does it. Avoid the strings on the upstroke for the time being. Just focus on using a **downstroke**.

Now count. Out loud. I mean it. Count "one, two, three, four; one, two, three, four…" as you strum. Over and over again. Listen to the sound you are making. *It's music.* Each time you count, you are playing a beat. When you complete a count of four, you have played one measure, a bar, of music. Keep going. Listen to the sweetness of the sound.

Count and strum **evenly**. This is important. Don't speed it up or slow it down. Not now, anyway. You can do that all you want when you get the hang of it. For right now, just concentrate on the rich sound you are making with simple, even downstrokes. When you get bored, that's good. It means you've mastered it, and you are ready to progress to the next step.

Now when you play the first beat—"the one," as musicians call it—add a little pizzazz. Strike the **one beat** faster and harder. Keep on counting, but count it "ONE!, two, three, four; ONE!, two, three, four…," accenting the first beat by playing it harder and shouting it out when you count it. Musicians call this **syncopation**. You are adding a bit of flavor, a rhythm on top of a rhythm. "Keep on truckin,' baby, keep on TRUCK-in,' ba-by! ONE!, two,

three, four, TRUCK-in' ba-by, ONE, two, three, four, TRUCK-in' ba-by…"
Out loud. It helps if you stomp your foot or wiggle your butt on the ONE. Put
some dance in your rhythm.

You getting the idea? Now let's move the accent to the **two beat**: one,
TWO!, three, four; one, TWO!, three, four; one, TWO!, three, four… Notice
how the music "feels" different? It is. There is an unexplainable change, like
rounding a corner into a different neighborhood. The "dance" changes. Again,
wiggle your butt, shrug a shoulder, or tap your foot while you accent the two
beat, and speak the two louder than the other beats.

You are still counting out loud, aren't you? Good. Now move the accent to
the third beat (one, two, THREE!, four; one, two, THREE!, four…). When
you are comfortable with that, move it to the fourth beat (one, two, three,
FOUR!; one, two, three, FOUR!…). Practice playing all four accents and pay
attention to how you feel when you change the accented beat. We're not done
with this exercise yet. Buckle up for an exciting ride.

This time, let's accent the one and the three: ONE!, two, THREE!, four;
ONE!, two, THREE!, four; ONE!, two, THREE!, four… Wiggle on the one
and the three—now you're dancing! Many styles of country and folk music use
this syncopation. Play around with it for a while, then move on to the next
syncopated convention, the two and the four.

UKE TIP

One of the greatest functions of the ukulele is using it to express how you feel,
how you hope, how you dream, how you love. Are you sad? A rhythm might help
you express that. Play around with the accents on the beats to explore how
rhythms match with moods.

All the rhythms we have so far explored can be doubled with an "and a": one, *and a* two, *and a* three, *and a* four; *and a* one, *and a* two, etc. Or, ONE, *and a* two, *and a* THREE, *and a* four… The "and a" is an **upstroke**. As you return your index finger to the top of the strings, let it grace against the strings to create the "and a." This is referred to as the **backbeat** by musicians, and it adds a whole new dimension to the rhythms you can create.

UKE TIP

I once saw a bumper sticker that read, "Friends Don't Let Friends Clap on the One and Three." What does that mean? Well, it means the person who affixed that sticker to their car bumper is an ardent rock 'n' roller with a sense of humor and disdain for folk music. See how you feel when you play one, TWO!, three, FOUR!; one, TWO!, three, FOUR!... There's a stridency there that says, "I'm gonna' raise a fuss, and I'm gonna' raise a holler!" Knock yourself out playing this syncopated rhythm to your heart's delight, but we've got a lot more to explore.

Count it out loud when you first try it. If you do so long enough, the ability to count without thinking will get into your DNA, and your life as a musician will improve greatly. So, for now, count out loud. It really is worth it.

A Word about Time Signatures

The rhythms we have been exploring are not the only rhythms in the world of music. So far, we have only played with what is called 4/4 time—four beats per measure, counted in quarter notes. There are other counts or time signatures, most commonly 3/4—the **waltz rhythm**—where only three beats are counted, and each one is a quarter note. Often these measures are counted ONE, two, three; ONE, two, three; or, conversely, oom, PAH, PAH; oom, PAH, PAH.

There are numerous ways to break up rhythms into patterns and many unusual time signatures, and as you develop your ukulele skills you may want to mine the Internet to find and explore them. But for now, let's get back to basics.

When we set out to accent one or two beats of a four-beat measure, we did it by increasing the volume and intensity of the downstroke of the index finger. But what if you didn't feel like that? What if you felt more like a tropical breeze on a sunny beach? There's a way to conjure that and other feelings you may wish to express. The next section will check out a few of them.

The Ukulele Player's Toolbox

The way to enjoy the best the ukulele has to offer is to build a toolbox of strums, picks, plucks, muffles, licks, and other doo-dads that you can access at the lightest whim when you play. When you learn a technique and practice it enough, you'll find it sneaking into your playing almost on its own. There's no greater satisfaction than playing something you can't believe you just played. That experience comes often when you've taken the time to toss a few items in your toolbox.

To that end, we'll survey a few strumming basics to build up your ukulele player's toolbox. Know this before we explore: *not everyone can conquer every strum*. Do not dismay if there is a strum you like but just can't get. It is a common experience. Who knows, someday when you least expect it, you'll find yourself playing a strum you thought you'd never learn. You may even well develop a strum that is yours and only yours. Just don't quit playing because a strum came up that baffles you. It happens to all of us. Nobody gets all the music.

The Thumb Stroke

The wide fleshy thumb, when graced across the strings, tends to separate the notes like boards on a picket fence. There's air between them. Instead of accenting, say, the first beat of a measure with an ardent stroke of the index finger, see what happens when you use the thumb to accent instead. **Thumb,** two, three, four. See how soft that sounds? The thumb has a gentle feel. Some Hawaiian players use the thumb primarily to conjure soft blowing breezes. Of course, you can use the thumb heavily and get a different feeling. Either way, try it out, practice it, own it. It's now part of your toolbox.

The Trill

Breaking up a single beat by rapidly moving the index finger back and forth across the strings is called a **trill**. Here's how to do it: try playing a "ONE!, two, three, four" syncopated measure but this time doubling the speed of the index finger on the one beat. Or play a continuous quick strum like a steady machine gun, and as you count, pulse your strum by accenting the one beat. This trill or "tremolo" usually breaks a beat into four sixteenth notes. It takes practice, but if you count out loud and do the same practice we did earlier in this chapter, making the accented beat sound, you will gain facility, and the trill will be a great addition to your toolbox.

Something I learned early in my ukulele career was that I could execute the trill more dramatically and error-free if I concentrated on the A string and did not worry about the other strings. They get strummed anyway, but if I'm not thinking about them, I found, I don't stumble on them either.

The index finger trill can be a very important part of your playing. Horse around with it, playing it at different speeds until you really "get" it. Later on, you'll need the trill when we study **glissando**—strumming while moving a note or chord.

The All Nails Strum

This strum uses all four fingernails on the downstroke and sometimes the thumb on the upstroke. It's a good strum for the "one and a" rhythm. You can let all four fingers cross the strings in unison or angle your hand so they cross the strings one after the other. It's a subtle difference, but it's still a difference. It gives a much richer sound than just the index finger. Playing around with this configuration often leads to interesting nuances that will pepper your playing.

The Roll Strum

With this strum, you unwind all four fingers, starting with the pinkie, then the ring, middle, and index fingers. Each finger hits the strings sequentially. It gives a beat with blurred edges, a sort of fat beat with a lot going on inside it. Flamenco guitar players use it, and it does give a bit of that flamenco flavor to your playing.

This stroke can be intensified by "throwing" it at the other strings—in other words, unrolling your fingers while simultaneously moving your arm downward, as though you are shaking water off your fingers. It adds a punch to it. You can also add a downward thumb stroke trailing along at the end of the roll. Both types are definitely worth having in your toolbox.

Now try using the All Nails Strum on three beats and end with the Roll Strum. By mixing the All Nails Strum and the Roll Strum this way, you may catch on to how easy it is to mix strums together. This too—the mixing of strums—should be in your toolbox.

The Back Roll

This is the reverse of the Roll Strum. Instead of rolling the fingers outward, they are rolled inward across the strings, like in a gathering motion. The hand stays still, but the fingers move. When this strum is used, the G string is the last one sounded. This gives the chord a slightly different personality, especially at the end of a tune. And it's fun.

The Strum and Muffle

The All Nails Strum and the Roll Strum can be muffled as they compete, resulting in what I call the Strum and Muffle. By muffling both strums, you cause a hypnotic pulse on top of the rhythm and syncopation. To do the Strum and Muffle, as you finish a downstroke on either strum, let the flat of your hand stop the strings for an instant before you start the next strum. Think of it not as a strum but a thump. Try this on for size: strum, thump, strum, thump, strum, thump, strum, thump… Think of the sound of a choo-choo train (which may be the original source of this rhythm). The ability to strum-thump is a ukulele toolbox "gotta have."

The Tickle

This one is sort of like the Back Roll, but it tends to occur over several beats. It's a fairly modern strum, used by several players. Some use two fingers, others three, to "tickle" the strings while the thumb is held against the body of the ukulele. This is to hold the hand steady above the strings while the fingers dance. It's tricky to do and maintain the beat, but persistence and practice can land this one in your toolbox. Significant players who use this technique are James Hill, Lil' Rev, and Ukulele Bartt. You can find all of them on the Internet.

The Figure 8 Stroke

The Figure 8 Stroke is a continuous movement making a sideways eight shape or an infinity sign. This stroke was popular in the 1920s. The player makes a figure eight across the front of the uke, gracing the strings on the way down where the neck meets the body, coming up across the strings at the neck, then crossing again where the neck meets the body. You strum **up** across the body and **down** at the neck-body juncture. This creates an interesting pulse and continuity. Any one of the paths across the strings can be accented by an increase of finger pressure as it moves through the path.

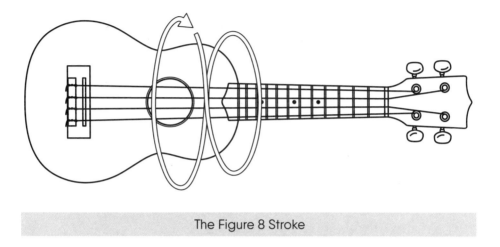

The Figure 8 Stroke

The Figure 8 Stroke is sometimes used in an ensemble when it's the ukulele's time to be in the background and keep a steady rhythm going. It can be cumbersome to play at first, but it's worth learning. Play it until you are comfortable with it, then try accenting one or two of the motions.

The Pinch Stroke

This stroke is not only rhythmic; it is also a "gateway stroke" to melody. (We'll get to more of that later.) You can quickly sound like an accomplished player with this strum. Simply pinch two strings on a beat instead of strumming. Try pinching the two outside strings (the G and A strings) and let them ring, like this: pinch, strum, strum, strum, pinch, strum, strum, strum… We'll explore this more in Chapter 4. But try it out now as a syncopation maneuver. And mess around with pinching different strings—you might find yourself writing a song!

The Plick

Not just a pick and not quite a pluck, this strum is a combination developed by me and is my signature strum. The middle and ring finger make a pedestal by resting on the top of the ukulele body just below the strings and soundhole. The thumb alternates plucks between the G and C strings while the index finger does a slow trill on the E and A strings. One way to learn it is to form the pedestal, then bobble the index finger across the E and A strings. When this feels natural, keep it going while alternately plucking the two top strings with the thumb slowly but in rhythm. A most useful tool for your toolkit!

The Split Stroke

This is one of two strums used by the British ukulele legend George Formby, still influential in England today. This strum has three parts—a strum down with the index finger, a pick up of the A string on the way back, followed by a pick down with the thumb on the G string. Formby often toggled the note on the A string to create a kind of rolling feeling. Many players have demonstrated Formby's peculiar strum. You can find them on *YouTube*.

UKULELE HEROES

J. Chalmers Doane, who started the Doane Method of music teaching, made it his mission to make sure every Canadian student received music education by the sixth grade. The Doane Uschool site is run by Chalmers's daughter, Melanie Doane. Visit their website at http://uschool.ca/.

The Thumb Roll

Formby's other distinctive strum is an up-down stroke, but the downstroke is followed by the thumb, which is held about three inches away from the index finger. Start out slowly, down with the index finger, followed by the thumb, and then an upstroke with the index finger. This strum is sometimes called the "triple strum" because of its three distinctive parts. Once you get the hang of it, bring it up to speed and enjoy the pulse it gives.

The Claw Hammer

This strum is based on an old-time banjo technique and is useful in many old folk and bluegrass tunes. With this strum, the player bends all four fingers into a claw on the strum hand, keeping the thumb nearby but not touching the fingers. Using the nail on the index finger, strike the C string, followed by an All Nails Strum, then use the thumb to pluck the G string. Some players call this the "Bum-Diddy" strum: "Bum" is the striking of the C note; "Did-" the full-on strum; and "-dy" the pluck of the G string. It takes some practice to get it into your DNA, but slow, steady practice will secure its place in your toolbox. Lil' Rev and Aaron Keim have *YouTube* videos of this technique.

A Final Word on Strumming

It should be obvious by now that strumming is the source of creating rhythm on the ukulele. Later, in Chapter 5, we will explore other techniques that contribute to rhythm and add personality to your playing. Remember, not everyone can do every strum, nor do they have to. Not every strum is appropriate to every song. Selecting a strum to use depends on what you are trying to say. Are you sad? In love? Awed by nature? Mad at politicians? Making fun? Blue at the loss of a favorite pet? There's a strum for that. You may have to make one up to fit your feeling. That's the job and the fun. Please don't kick yourself because there's a strum you seem not to conquer. You'll find another that will work.

In this section, we stayed with a one-finger chord. In the next chapter, we explore multifinger chords, harmony, and finally, playing songs.

Chapter 3

HARMONY

In this chapter we'll cover the next basic element of music: **harmony**. Harmony is when a group of notes are played together simultaneously and the resulting sound is pleasing to the ear. Musical harmony is expressed in **chords**. Most songs are made up of two or three chords, sometimes more. In general, chords make up the background tapestry of a song and are controlled by the rhythm.

In this chapter we'll explore a variety of chords. We will learn how chords are built and how they're used, and then we will start building up a chord vocabulary to continue filling up that toolbox.

Understanding Chords

Think of chords as the building blocks of songs. Chords are usually made up of three notes, or **tones**, but sometimes they can contain four or five. There are **major** and **minor** chords. Recall the one-finger chord we used in Chapter 2. Let's take a deeper look at it.

The name of this chord is C major or, simply, C. The three notes of the major chord are called:

- The **root** tone (also called the **tonic**, or **one**)
- The **mediant** tone (also called the **third**)
- The **dominant** tone (also called the **fifth**)

If we think of the Do-Re-Mi scale from our childhood, the **root**, **mediant**, and **dominant** notes correspond to the **Do**, **Mi**, and **So** notes in the scale—the **first**, **third**, and **fifth** notes in that scale.

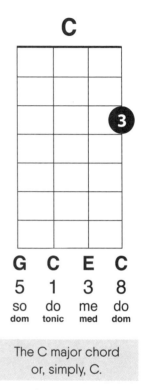

C

G	C	E	C
5	1	3	8
so	do	me	do
dom	tonic	med	dom

The C major chord or, simply, C.

UKE TIP

The Do-Re-Mi scale is just another way of denoting the standard musical scale of letter notes as syllables:

C D E F G A B C = Do Re Mi Fa So La Ti Do

People thought it was easier to remember the notes this way.

Chord names begin with the name of the root tone. The root tone is the primary tone upon which the chord is built and establishes the scale on which it is based. In the case of the C major chord we've been looking at, the letter names of the C major chord would be **C**, **E**, and **G**, which are the first, third, and fifth notes of the **C scale**.

The root tone also establishes the key that is used to build other chords within the same family of chords. It's easy to understand how chords are built when you understand the terminology used when adding notes to the basic "1-3-5" spelling of a major chord.

Take a look at the diagram showing the names of several C-based chords.

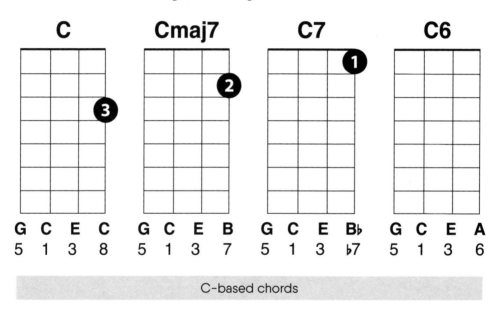

C-based chords

Now let's learn how to play them:

- **C Chord:** *To play the C chord, place the ring finger on the third fret of the A string.* This makes a C note. It helps to think of this as moving the nut up three frets on that string.
- **Cmaj7 Chord:** *To play the Cmaj7 chord, place the middle finger on the second fret.* This makes a B note. The B note is the seventh note in the scale of C.

- **C7 Chord:** *To play the C7 chord, place the index finger on the first fret.* This makes a B♭ note (pronounced "B-flat"). A B♭ note is flattened, or diminished, or is the minor seventh note in the scale of C.
- **C6 Chord:** *Now we've arrived at the tuning of the ukulele itself, GCEA.* For the C6 chord, the A string is left open. The A is the sixth note in the C scale.

Take some time now to practice playing the C, Cmaj7, C7, and C6 chords on your ukulele. Notice how the simple movement of fingers "retreating" from the C note each give a distinct flavor to the chord.

When first learning the ukulele, you likely will stick to the C or C7 chords. As you progress, especially if you experiment with jazz, you'll probably find yourself using the Cmaj7 or C6 chord. But get the basics down first. As your playing progresses, you can always come back to this chapter for ideas. On this first reading, it's important not to let all this complexity discourage and distract you. Keep it simple for now.

Major versus Minor

New players often get confused—with good reason—by musical terminology. *Major* and *minor* are two terms that come up a lot in music and are important to understand. For instance, in a major chord, like the C major chord we've been looking at, the third is a major third. What does that mean?

In the context of the scale of C, D, E, F, G, A, B, C, the third (third note) is an E, a major note. Because it uses major notes, the C major chord is a **major chord**. Now if we "flatten" the E by using an E♭ ("E-flat") instead, the third is now a "minor third." (Some musicians call a minor third a "flat three." Don't be confused—it means the same thing.) The chord is now a **minor chord**.

Another word musicians use for "flat" is **diminished**. A flattened note is indicated by using the flat symbol, which looks like a lowercase b. For example, in the C6♭5 chord, the chord is a C6, but the five note (a G) has been flattened to a G♭. (I don't know why anyone would want to do that, but that's how it would be spelled.)

UKULELE HEROES

The Mighty Uke: The Amazing Comeback of a Musical Underdog is a full-length documentary movie by Tony Coleman that features players from around the world. A must-see for ukulele players. Learn more about it at www .mightyukemovie.com/.

There is one type of chord in which *all* the notes, except the root tone, are diminished. Curiously, it's called a "diminished" chord. The symbol for such a chord is a °. For example, a C diminished chord would be shown as C°.

Some chords feature an **augmented** note, a note that is sounded a fret higher. An augmented note is the opposite of a diminished note. The symbol for that is a + sign, so that a C chord with an augmented five note is sometimes written C+5. Since the five note is most often the note that is raised, modern musicians simply use the spelling C+, and the five is understood. Some might prefer to use the terminology "sharp five." Again, it means the same thing.

Confused yet? Well, let's muck it up even more. A string or note can be considered out of tune when it is flat or sharp but can be perfectly in tune if it is a flat or sharp note! For example, an E♭ note could be out of tune, either sharp or flat. The name and the condition use the same terminology, sometimes confusing new players. An E♭ is the note between D and E, but a flat E♭ note is not quite high enough in pitch!

So, in summary: **both chords and scales can be major or minor**. As we've seen in the case of chords, major becomes minor by flattening the note, so a Cm chord (C minor) is made of C, E♭, and G (one, a flattened three, and the five). In a scale, the same kind of thing happens—the third note is flattened, and sometimes others are. We will get to that in Chapter 4.

For now, rest assured that you don't need to know all of this to play the ukulele at this moment, but if you want to keep getting better at it, it's good to understand.

One, Four, Five

It's time to play your first song on the ukulele. It goes like this: "Tap tapa tap tap, tap—Tap Tap!" Play it by tapping your index finger or thumb on the top of your ukulele. Do you hear it? The music, I mean. Play it again, but now add the lyrics. Sing, "Shave and a haircut, two bits." Even though you are only playing a piece of wood with one tone, do you not hear it has rhythm, movement, and even lyrics?

Now play the same thing while holding the C chord. "Shave and a haircut, two bits." Play it a few times. You might notice that even though you are playing only one chord, your ear seems to be filling in what is missing—harmonic movement and melody.

Now let's introduce the G7 chord into our musical project. Counting up from C, the five chord ("fifth") is G, the dominant note in the scale of C. Very often, but not always, the five chord is played with a flat seventh in it to give the chord a bit more suspense. We'll talk about that in a while, but for now let's just play this two-chord song.

Check out the chords in the illustration and play them a few times.

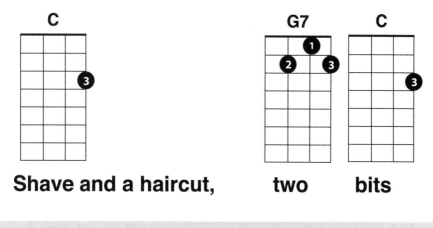

Shave and a haircut,   two   bits

The "Shave and a Haircut" song with two chords—C and G7.

There are literally tens of thousands of songs that use just these two chords, the C and G7. From Hank Williams's "Jambalaya (On the Bayou)" to the more recent "Achy Breaky Heart," Chuck Berry's "Memphis, Tennessee," "Tom Dooley," and other folk tunes the world over.

♫

UKE TIP

One time I complained to my friend Buddy about how many bad notes I played during my solos. He said, "Dan, you're never more than one fret away from a note that *will* work." He was right. Eventually I learned to stretch bad notes into good ones by pulling on the string or sliding into an adjacent fret. In time, it became somewhat second nature. (I still mess up enough, but nobody gets hurt.) Miles Davis said, "It's not the note you play that's the wrong note—it's the note you play afterwards that makes it right or wrong."

An *interval* is the distance between two notes (more on this in the next chapter). When you add a flat five interval to a major chord, you create a tension that really wants to go home, that wants to resolve. Play the two-chord "Shave and a Haircut" song again. Now play it but stop after you play the G7, at the word "two." Can you keep from finishing it? Don't you want to? That's the tension I'm talking about—the tension that drives music and makes it want to come to a conclusion.

To hear the flat five interval, make a G7 chord and strike the E string and A string alternately. Notice how it sounds like a French ambulance? Danger. Something is wrong. It's gotta be fixed. Do an energetic trill strum on the G7 chord. Can you stand it? Can you feel the suspense, the yearning to run to the safety of home? There's the source of tension. That's why so many songwriters use seventh chords to help make their music move.

UKE TIP

Getting used to the G7 chord might take some practice. Try practicing this way: start out with the ring finger on the second fret of the A string, your index finger on the first fret of the E string, and your middle finger on the second fret of the C string. Once you have made this "triangle" shape with your fingers, lift it off the fretboard, then place it down a few times. Now practice sliding from the G7 chord to the C by simply sliding your ring finger to the third fret, while lifting the other two. Do this a few times, then play the tune. Use the index finger of your strumming hand to play a downstroke on the word "shave," then a down-up stroke on the "and a," and two downstrokes for "haircut." Pause for a beat, then strum a downstroke each for "two" and "bits."

Now let's discuss the I-IV-V chord progression, a common chord progression in music. Chord progressions are simply series of chords played in progression. The numbers refer to the chords in the key: the one (I), four (IV), and five (V). Recognizing and practicing common chord progressions is key and will help you once you start playing with other musicians.

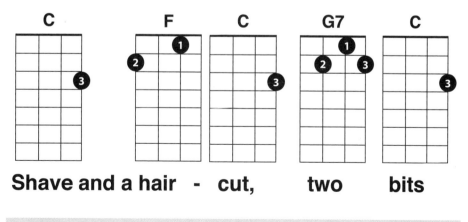

Same song but now with two additional chords—the F and G7 chords.

The other most common chord used in a song is the **four chord**. Some have called it the "sunshine chord" or the "Amen chord." (Play a trill on an F chord while singing "A-a-a-a" and then "men" on the C chord. See why they call it the "Amen chord"?) Let's add it to our little song.

To make an F chord, put your index finger on the first fret of the E string and your middle finger on the second fret of the G string. This version of the F chord has two As, one on the G string and, of course, one on the A string. The C string is the five note, and the E string is the first fret where the F lives. If you drop your ring finger on the third fret of the A string, you still have an F chord, spelled F, A, C, but now you have two Cs—one of them an octave higher—rather than two As. When playing this song, play one beat of F on the word "hair," then go to the C chord. Notice that the song does not feel like it went "home" when it left the F chord. When you finish up with the "two bits" of G7 and C, you'll hear it resolve. That's music.

UKE TIP

The G7 chord, like all seventh chords, has a dissonant interval in it that adds suspense to it. There's already a tension in the five chord, even if it's played as a major chord. There's something about the five that wants to "go home," in other words, get back to the root chord. We say "Do-Re-Mi" all the time without feeling the need to continue. We're okay with "Do-Re-Mi-Fa" too. But with "Do-Re-Mi-Fa-So," there's a strong urge to finish it.

We start out with the home chord, C, introduce a bit of sunshine with the F chord, then give it a quick "turnaround" of G7 and C. Many musicians end their songs with it and call it the five-one turnaround. At other times, when musicians want to return to the beginning of a song after finishing it once, they will add a five-seven chord to return them to the top.

Now here's an interesting thing: another use of the flatted seven is to add it to the tonic chord, the home chord, because it leads to the four chord! Just as G is the five of C, C is the five of F. The F scale has one flat in it, unlike C, which has no flats or sharps (no black keys on the piano). The F scale reads F, G, A, B♭, C, D, E, F. When you are playing a C chord and follow it with a C7 chord, you really have no choice but to go to an F, the "home" chord of C7. To test it out, play the three chord "Shave and a haircut, two bits" tune with a C7 chord on "and a": C, C7, F, C, G7, C. We don't really need it in our "two bits" ditty, but it does work. In some songs it works really well, setting up a tension that needs resolution.

For just a moment, make the one-finger C chord. Notice how your index and middle fingers make a peace sign extended out from the neck of the ukulele? Rotate your hand upward and place those two fingers on the fretboard while lifting your ring finger at the same time. Check out the two-finger F chord diagram to see where to locate your fingers.

Notice that this F chord has two A notes in it. Even though they are the same tone, they will have different sounds, due to the "timbre" of an open string and one that is fretted. And the chance they will be in perfect tune with one another is pretty slim. This slight difference of two notes in unison, a result of the re-entrant tuning, gives the ukulele its distinctive sweet sound.

Practice going from the C to F chords, C to G7, F to G7, and so on. Try out the strums we explored in the last chapter. Play several measures of each chord and always end a sequence on the C chord. Perhaps you will hear a song you recognize or make one up.

Following are a few common songs to help you "keep Keepin' On."

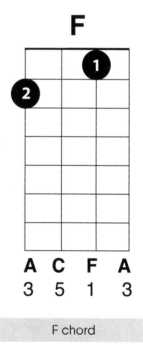

F

A	C	F	A
3	5	1	3

F chord

Buffalo Gals

(1844)

```
  C    F      C              G7           C
As I was lumb'ring down the street, down the street, down the street
```

```
              F    C              G7          C
A handsome gal I chanced to meet, oh, she was fair to view
```

```
C      G7           C
Buffalo gals, can't you come out tonight,
```

```
        G7                        C
Can't you come out tonight, can't you come out tonight?
```

```
      G7             C
Buffalo gals can't you come out tonight
```

```
      G7                    C
And dance by the light of the moon.
```

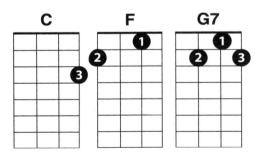

This song has been around for 173 years. In the early years, towns adopted it as their own, adapting the words as they saw fit. By 1848, it had jelled into "Buffalo Gals" (after Buffalo, New York). Play it a few times, make up your own words, or try reversing the G7 and F chords to see how the movement of the tune changes. Give yourself permission to goof around.

Oh! Susanna

(1848)

```
      C                                        G7
Oh, I came from Alabama with a banjo on my knee
```

```
        C                               G7   C
I'm goin' to Louisiana, my true love for to see
```

```
                                               G7
It rained all night the day I left, the weather it was dry
```

```
        C                          G7            C
The sun so hot I froze to death, Susanna don't you cry.
```

```
F              C           G7
Oh Susanna, oh don't you cry for me
```

```
      C                                 G7    F
I've come from Alabama with a banjo on my knee
```

```
F              C           G7
Oh Susanna, oh don't you cry for me
```

```
      C                                 G7    F
I've come from Alabama with a banjo on my knee
```

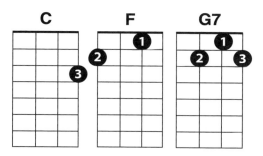

This is the song that set off popular music. Stephen Foster published it in 1848, and it was sung the following year by folks who flocked to the California gold rush. This version is the simplest version to play.

57

Home on the Range

(1872)

```
      F        F7            Bb
Oh, give me a home where the buffalo roam,

        F                    C7
Where the deer and the antelope play,

      F        F7       Bb
Where seldom is heard a discouraging word

        F           C7      F
And the skies are not cloudy all day.


C7                  F
Home, home on the range!

                       C7
Where the deer and the antelope play,

      F                  Bb
Where seldom is heard a discouraging word,

        F           C7      F
And the skies are not cloudy all day.
```

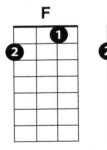

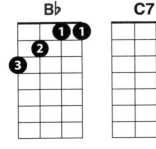

Written in 1872 by Kansas pharmacist Dr. Brewster Higley, this tune is a favorite campfire song and has been declared the most popular country song of all time. Another version appears in Chapter 6.

58

Playing chords rhythmically is the ukulele player's first and main job. This is why we've filled your toolbox first with a collection of strums (rhythm) and then a whole catalog of chords and ways to play them. You've now landed in one of the primary growth spaces for ukulele players—a space you could swim around in for years. *The learning process never ends.* I've been playing the ukulele for more than sixty years, and I still discover new ways and places on the neck to play chords that had eluded me before. The excitement of discovery never ends.

Chapter 8 lists many chords in many ways they can be played, including common patterns they follow. Take the time once in a while to check them out, with your ukulele in your hand. Now is not too early to visit Chapter 8. (But make sure you come back to the next chapter!) Get the chords into your toolbox as well as their patterns. If you do, you can use them on a whim.

You now have several chords under your belt. Make up your own song, with words or not. Many players find themselves "noodling"—just strumming around and picking on chords and "licks" they know. Leave your ukulele out where you can grab it whenever you walk by (but not where you can sit on it). Play your noodle tune and walk on. You just practiced. And that's what it takes—practice.

UKULELE HEROES

Australian uke player Azo Bell began playing ukulele in 1992, after two and a half decades as a professional musician. Today, he brings great energy to jazz tunes, including spinning his ukulele in the air and catching it without missing a beat. Visit his website at https://azobell.bandcamp.com/.

Chapter 4

MELODY

Now let's turn to melody. Melody is the song in your head, the remembered tune, the part of a song you whistle, hum, or sing. Melody is usually a pleasant series of single notes that hang out together, leap and hop, or linger awhile. It's the part of a song you take with you. Intervals, scales, and note duration make music "move" horizontally—that's melody.

Learning Melodies

In no particular order, here are the ways to learn melodies:

- **Make them up!** Yes, you have permission to do this. Pick random notes at random durations. If you hear something that intrigues you, repeat it. Then, alter it. Mess around and enjoy it. Have a lyric in mind? Explore other sequences of notes that go along with it. Make up a song. It's all yours.

- **Listen to recordings and hunt for the melody on your ukulele.** Not everyone has the ear for this, but it's always worth trying. To try, listen for the resolution in the song to determine its key, then work the scale of notes of that key. Eventually, most folks get better at it, especially when they've had a success or two. Always worth trying—but only if you relax and enjoy it!

- **Learn and watch from someone who knows.** Watch their fingers as they play. Ask them to repeat the part you didn't understand. Most musicians are happy to show you what they know. Teaching others makes us all better players. It helps to learn the chord sequence first, then pick out the melody within the chords. Melody lines are often in the chords.

- **Learn to read sheet music.** You don't have to be a speed reader, but you can verify how a song goes, one note at a time. If you learn several notes that make a phrase, play it repeatedly until you "own" it. Then, move on to the next phrase. Then, add them together and play the new extended phrase repeatedly. Continue until you've made the whole song your own. Revisit the song once in a while so it stays fresh in your mind—and fingers.

- **Learn tablature.** Not quite sheet music, tablature is a form of musical notation that shows the fingering instead of the pitch. Tablature specialized for ukulele displays the four strings (for a standard guitar it would display six strings) as lines, and which fret is played on them in which order. There are "tabs" for most songs on the Internet. They are especially good when you think you have a song down but are unsure of a phrase or two. Look up the tab and verify how it goes.

- **Watch lessons on *YouTube*.** Many musicians love to show others how to play their favorite tune by making a video and posting it to the Internet. The song you seek might be there. Search for it.
- **Imply melodies by picking notes of the scale from within the chords.** Not everyone gets to be Chet Atkins or Andrés Segovia—musicians who effortlessly find the chords and play melodies at the same time. The rest of us, though, can have fun playing around with the melody and can rely on our ears (and our audiences') to fill in what's missing. This technique requires you to learn scales and where the notes are on the ukulele fretboard. Later in this chapter we will take a closer look at this technique.

Scales

Do, Re, Mi, Fa, So, La, Ti, Do. When young, friends and I could chant this scale at will. For years, I thought it was the *only* musical scale. Later, as I fancied myself a ukulele player, I had a hard time jamming with rock and rollers. Nothing I did seemed to work with what they were playing. I could play the proper chords, but when I tiptoed into "taking a lead," I was at a loss.

One day I was jamming with my brother Billy, an accomplished rock and surf guitarist. He was all over the neck, and everything seemed correct. "Billy," I pleaded, "what are you doing?"

"I'm just playing the blues scale," Billy said, matter of fact.

"Blues scale?" I queried. "What's that?"

He showed me a very simple box pattern on the guitar. It was not Do-Re-Mi. It was something else. He taught it to me in the next five minutes, and a whole new world opened up for me. (I think it was my reward for teaching him "Pipeline," "Walk, Don't Run," and "Mr. Moto" when he was ten years old.) I soon learned there are many scales, and each one opened a new avenue of musical pleasure. I was a decent rhythm player but fearful of stretching out into the world of soloing and improvisation. I could not throw caution to the wind and play from the heart. I was literally shackled by a strict adherence to the only scale I knew.

I wouldn't wish that experience on anyone else, so in this chapter we will explore a few common scales. You do not need to know every kind of scale to play the ukulele, and you aren't expected to master them now, but it's good to be aware that different scales exist. Just knowing that scales and modes (starting a scale on a note other than the one) exist gives you territory to explore when you feel like stepping out.

Chromatic versus Diatonic

In Western music there are only twelve notes, though they repeat. A **chromatic scale** includes all the notes, each a half step apart. This twelve-note scale is called *chromatic*. On the piano, it includes both the black (sharp or flat) and the white ("natural") keys, from one C to the next: C, C♯ (or D♭), D, D♯ (or E♭), E, F, F♯ (or G♭), G, G♯ (or A♭), A, A♯ (or B♭), B (and C again).

Since the root of the word *chromatic* is *color*, I reckon it means this scale has the whole palette of musical colors in it.

Notice there is no sharp or flat note between **B** and **C**, or **E** and **F**. (There's no black key between these keys on the piano, either.) Remember this with the aid of "**B**ig **C**ats **E**at **F**ish."

If we don't include black keys, we get C, D, E, F, G, A, B, C, or Do-Re-Mi, etc. We can also recite it as 1, 2, 3, 4, 5, 6, 7, 8. This scale, or sequence of notes, is the **diatonic scale** or, simply, the **major scale**. There is a whole tone between each note, except between E and F (the 3 and 4) and between B and C (the 7 and 8).

Confused? Look at the following illustration. It shows the C scales in several ways, including their positions on the ukulele in tablature form.

The top block is a musical score that shows the chromatic scale in the key of C—all twelve notes, including the "accidentals," or black notes, on the piano. The note names below show the diatonic C scale. The next block shows the corresponding numerical position of the diatonic scale, followed by the Do-Re-Mi syllables. The final graph is common tablature format for the ukulele. The lines represent the ukulele strings (top line always shows the bottom string, the thinnest string), and the numbers tell you which fret to play a note. Tablature is a good way to learn or check the melody of a song.

C scales in tablature form for the ukulele.

Now let's turn to octaves. Octaves are the eight notes in a scale. The following image shows the two octaves of the C scale on the ukulele. The scale shows the note names and their numeric position. Notes of the C scale are elsewhere on the neck, but this illustration shows the most direct way to play the two octaves.

The neck usually joins the body at the twelfth fret, which is where each string completes a scale. Notice that the A string goes from an open A to the A on the twelfth fret. Playing just those notes from A to A is the **Am scale**. It is a very good idea to memorize the note locations on the A string—it will serve as a roadmap when you begin playing farther up the neck. We'll talk more about this in Chapter 8.

The spaces between the notes of the major diatonic scale can be described as whole step, whole step, half step, whole step, whole step, whole step, half step or, simply, WWHWWWH.

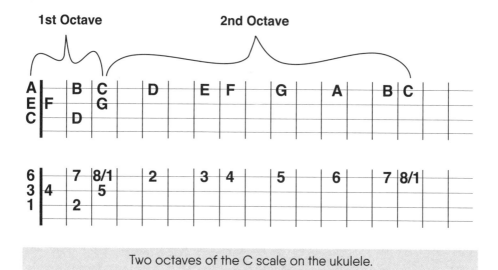

Two octaves of the C scale on the ukulele.

An important thing to remember is that this "geometry" of a scale, or sequence of notes, does not alter with a change in key. For example, when playing the Do-Re-Mi scale for G, the geometry follows the alphabet until you get to the seventh note: G, A, B, C, D, E, F♯, G. The seventh note is F♯. It just happens that the half step between the 3 and 4 falls on the B and C, but the 7 has to be bumped up to an F♯ to keep the geometry correct.

♪

UKE TIP

Dead center in the diatonic scale, but not part of it, is a note that is three whole steps from the root note, the **tritone**. Three whole steps: C to D, D to E, E to F♯. A very discomforting sound. Three more whole steps, F♯ to G♯, G♯ to A♯, A♯ to C, give the same discomfort. If you think of the tritone as a pivot in the scale, you can understand the first part of the scale as whole, whole, half; then the "pivot"; then, starting at the next note, the five, the pattern is again whole, whole, half. The tritone interval of three full tones gives seventh and diminished chords a dissonance and suspense that demand resolution.

The Relative Minor, Naturally

Every major key has a **minor scale** associated with it, based on **the sixth note in its scale**. In the key of C, the sixth is A. If you play the notes of the C scale, but from A to A, you will be playing the Am scale: A, B, C, D, E, F, G, A. The geometry changes from the C major scale. The half steps between B and C, and between E and F, move to different spots in the scale. Instead of coming after two whole steps, the third note, C, shows up after a step and a half. This is referred to as a **minor third** or flat third. There is also a half step now between the fifth and the sixth, making the sixth a minor 6. The scale ends with a whole step between the G and A, rather than a half step, as in the major scale. This type of scale, all whole steps, except for the minor 3 and 6, is also called the **natural minor scale**.

Remember, using only the natural notes of the C scale, but starting and ending on the A note, we were able to create the Am natural minor scale. That's because A is the sixth note in the C major scale. C is the sixth note in the scale of E♭, so to make a Cm natural scale we start on C and go through the E♭ scale to the next C. It looks like this:

C, D, E♭, F, G, A♭, B♭, C

It's a good idea to think through this minor scale stuff. It's often a source of confusion for new musicians. It behooves you to look at it again. The C major scale and the Cm scale have different notes in them.

♫

UKE TIP

Some musicians consider Cm to be the key of E♭, because Cm is the relative minor of E♭. Similarly, the Am scale is really in the key of C, since its notes are based on the C major scale. Think Einstein—"It's relative"! Same idea.

The Harmonic Minor Scale

The harmonic minor scale is the same as the natural relative minor scales derived from major scales but without the lowered seventh note. The A harmonic minor scale reads:

$$A, B, C, D, E, F, G\sharp, A$$

This gives the otherwise natural minor scale a penultimate leading tone to help top off the scale.

The Melodic Minor Scale

The melodic minor has an "up" and a "down." As the scale goes up, only the third and the sixth are lowered. The C melodic minor scale going up is C, D, E♭, F, G, A♭, B, C. But going down, the third, sixth, and seventh notes are flattened: C, B♭, A♭, G, F, E♭, D, C. This scale "pulls" toward the top when played up and drags downward on the way back. Again, a person doesn't need to know all this to play the ukulele, but sometimes knowing some of the conventions at work in a song increases the enjoyment of it. If you find it confusing, forget about it and just play.

The Harmonic Chord Scale

For ease of understanding, we'll stick to the C scale, but what is true of this scale applies to all the other keys as well. When a piano player plays a C chord, comprised of C, E, and G, he or she plays every other white key, starting with the C note. Keeping the same three-finger configuration but starting with the next higher note, the player sounds a Dm chord. Continuing up the keyboard in this fashion, the complete harmonic scale is played: C, Dm, Em, F, G, Am, B°, and C again. (Diminished chords require four notes, so the B° is not a complete chord but contains the three natural notes in it. The fourth note, G♭, is not played in this scenario.)

Repetitive playing of the harmonic scale is a good way to train your ears and fingers. The chords of the harmonic scale are commonly used in songs. Here's a great thing: every note in every chord of the harmonic scale is a note that is in the major diatonic scale of that key. Therefore, you can access chunks of the scale at all times when playing or implying the melody. Every note you pick is at least a harmony note in the key. This gives you permission to experiment. Sometimes a song will leave the scale for a unique effect. If you are familiar with the harmonic scale as well as the scale of the key you are in, you have a much better chance to hear a foreign note and step outside the scale to play it.

The Pentatonic Scale

This scale is based on the regular scale but uses only five of its notes—the 1, 2, 3, 5, 6, plus the octave. Thus, the C pentatonic scale is C, D, E, G, A, C. This is one of the scales used heavily in rock and roll and blues.

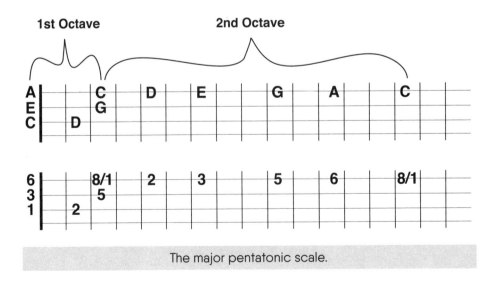

The major pentatonic scale.

Have fun playing this major pentatonic scale in a random order, starting and ending on a C note. Sometimes it's hard to stop. Because the major pentatonic scale doesn't use the 4 or 7 (F and B), there are no half steps in it. Some theorists say this is why any note of this scale works well with any major chord progression. The pentatonic and blues scales are great fun to play with reckless abandon.

♫

UKE TIP

To get a good feel for the pentatonic scale, visit Bobby McFerrin's demonstration on *YouTube* at www.youtube.com/watch?v=ne6tB2KiZuk.

The Minor Pentatonic

The minor pentatonic is based on the natural minor scale, but only the 1, 3, 4, 5, and 7 are used. The 2 and 6 are left out. Thus, the C minor pentatonic scale reads C, E♭, F, G, B♭, C. The D and A♭ are omitted. The first position on the ukulele for this scale is a cinch to learn. It forms a sort of "box" from the nut to the third fret. That box can be moved around the neck to pick out notes that sound good with various chords. Practice it so you can play it anywhere on the neck. We'll visit this again in Chapter 8.

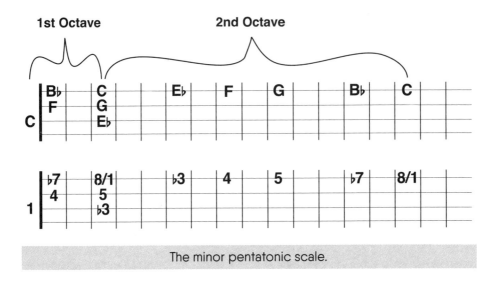

The minor pentatonic scale.

The preceding illustration shows the box formation of the minor pentatonic in the key of C. Notice that some notes in the minor pentatonic scale are flattened: ♭3, ♭5, ♭7. Play these notes with a bluesy feeling in any order, but end on one of the C notes before you start a new phrase. To play this box in a different key, place your ring finger on the A string that has the root note of the key you want to be in, then bar all four strings three frets behind it (toward the nut). You have effectively moved the nut to a new location and can play the box in its new position.

The Blues Scale

This scale is the same as the minor pentatonic but includes the tritone. In the key of C, this is C, E♭, F, G♭, G, B♭, C. The G♭ (or F♯) is called the "blue note." It gets played whenever the player feels like it. Simple as that.

The tritone is added to the minor pentatonic scale to produce the blues scale. In the key of C, this is F♯ or G♭. Try playing a C chord for a couple of measures, then pick around this scale for a measure or two, then go back to the C chord. Do the same with F and G7 chords. In Chapter 8 we'll explore the blues a bit more.

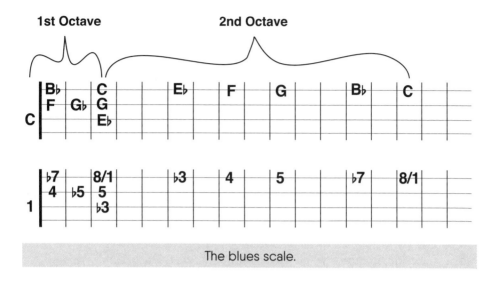

The blues scale.

It is not unusual for an accomplished blues player to temporarily leave the blues scale and play chromatic and diatonic runs between notes of the blues scale. The blues scale is very forgiving for experimenting on the fly and gives players permission to improvise in a variety of ways. Be careful—it can be very addictive.

Intervals

Many musicians prefer to speak of **intervals**, or the distance between two notes. For example, the distance between C and G is a fifth, or perfect fifth. The distance between C and D is a second, but the distance between C and D♭ is a minor second. In the study of scales, one might simply go up the scale and back down again. In the study of intervals, however, the musician or singer studies the jump between different notes in the scale, say, the jump from C to G (a jump of five) or from C to the next C (an octave jump). *Learning to hear intervals is as important as learning scales.*

Try playing an open string followed by the note on the first fret. In a way, it doesn't matter what the names of the notes are—the interval is a minor two.

Play any note on the fretboard and the one next to it—a minor two. Play two frets away; it's a major two. A melody might go from the four note to the five note, but the interval is a major two because there's an empty fret between them. Some gifted musicians have the ability to play by following the intervals rather than the scale. It's a growth space for most of us.

Sometimes familiar tunes are used to identify intervals. An example is the "Here Comes the Bride" song, in which the first two words make a perfect fourth interval (C to F). Another famous interval is the "some-where" octave jump at the beginning of "Somewhere Over the Rainbow." In interval-speak, the unison one, the fourth, fifth, and octave are considered "perfects" and when sharpened or flattened are said to be augmented or diminished. The other intervals are considered minor when flattened, major when left natural. Recognizing intervals when you hear them is a talent unto itself and is sometimes equated with having "perfect pitch." Not everyone has it, but it's worth trying.

UKULELE HEROES

Ken Middleton is a Brit who represents Ohana ukuleles and travels the world giving ukulele lessons at festivals. He is an ardent contributor of ukulele tunes on *YouTube*. Follow him at www.kenmiddleton.co.uk.

Chords and Scales

One of the great growth spaces for ukulele players is learning to mix melody lines and chords with ease. Doing so requires you to know the scale and the chords, and to have control of the strum, plucks, and picks in your ukulele toolbox.

UKULELE HEROES

Langley Ukulele Ensemble is an ever-changing group of high school students in British Columbia directed by Peter Luongo. They have appeared numerous times at the Honolulu International Festival. James Hill is an alumnus. Read about them at www.langleyukes.com/president-peter-luongo.

Inside Picking

At first, you learn scales by playing the notes in sequence: up the scale and back down again, over and over. Then you go on to play the scale in combinations: instead of CDEFGABC, you might play CDE, DEF, EFG, FGA, GAB, ABC, backward and forward. Practice this. Play random notes, but keep it logical by ending on a C note from time to time. And above all, make sure to keep it fun, not work!

Here's the next leap in conquering the scale: hold the primary chords that appear in the key you are playing, one at a time. In the key of C, start with the C, F, and G7 chords. While holding each of these chords, pick each note of the scale you can without lifting your finger. What we are trying to do here is train your fingers to know where the good spots are. Once you've played all the scale notes you can, lift your finger and play the notes you couldn't reach before. Go back to the chord.

Practice playing the notes of the scale and lifting your chording fingers and putting them back immediately. You don't have to play a song. You are just trying to get your fingers to know their way around the neighborhood.

Continue doing this exercise with each of the other chords. In time, you should be able to find the scale notes with each of the chords of the harmonic chord scale. In the key of C, every open string is a note in the scale, and every note in every chord in the harmonic chord scale is a note in the scale. They all count, but in this exercise, we want to be able to reach the other notes in the scale that are not being fretted at the time. For example, in a Dm chord, we should be able to hold the chord and still reach the G, B, and C notes on the E and A strings. (Don't forget to lift the Dm chord and play the scale notes under it, then make the chord again.) Keep this in mind: with this exercise, we are just trying to train our fingers and ears to *know* where things are.

Implying the Melody

Here's an oft-forgotten truth that, when remembered, can lead to great enjoyment: you don't have to play the entire melody! You can play around the melody and call it jazz. You can "croon" the tune, improvise on it. Since you have been ardently training your fingers to find the scale in the previous exercise, you have the ability to tickle the melody while you chord the song.

You know those paragraphs you see on *Facebook* and other places that start out "If u cn rd ths…"? Our brains fill in the missing vowels. The same thing happens when you play snippets of the melody or harmony in time, on time. The brain and our familiarity with the song fill in what is missing. Jazz players do it all the time. Give yourself permission to try it.

UKE TIP

Jazz pianist Jim Lowe said the main difference between a classical and jazz musician was that the former's task was to play exactly what the composer had written, and the latter's job was to get as far away from the melody as possible without losing it. The rest of us get our kicks just hinting at the melody as best we can while keeping the rhythm and harmony going smoothly. This usually takes an adventurist attitude and a toolbox of strums and picks.

To get an idea of what it takes to imply a melody, consider the old folk song "Oh My Darling, Clementine":

Oh my darling, oh my darling, oh my darling, Clementine
You are lost and gone forever, dreadful sorry, Clementine.

We could play this with a very simple strum. Four beats per measure. Start with a C chord, go to a G7 chord on "–tine" at the end of the first line, and hold that chord until "–tine" at the end of the second line. The melody of this tune travels up the A string and back, but we are not going to play it. But we will imply it.

Oh my darling, oh my darling, oh my darling, Clementine

You are lost and gone forever, dreadful sorry, Clementine

Oh My Darling, Clementine

Strum through this couplet several times to establish its rhythm while singing it out loud or in your head. As you continue playing, try replacing a strum beat with a picked note or with three quickly picked notes (a triplet) by using both the thumb and index finger of the strumming hand. If you play it smoothly enough, you will hear parts of the melody flavoring your strum.

Play the chords and sing the lyrics a few times through until you get the hang of it. When you've had enough fun doing that, instead of strumming at the end of the first "darling," try picking a note on any string on the "–ing" part of the word. In other words, do this: strum, strum, strum, pick, strum, strum, strum, pick. You may notice the pick falls on the "–ing" both times. Try playing just this phrase ("oh my darling, oh my darling") a few times, picking a different string each time you get to the "–ing." Do you notice that you seem to be playing the melody? Or at least the harmony part of it? When you think you've got the idea, go ahead and play the remainder of the couplet, picking a random note on the fourth beat or whenever you feel like it. If you do this often enough, you will hear the melody pop up, even though you are not playing it.

It's one of the wonders of music, and it's a great way to discover your own interpretation of songs you love. It's one of the best ways to make a song your own. Enjoy.

Chapter 5

DOO-DADS

Now that we've covered the basics—rhythm, harmony, and melody—

we're ready to move on to the techniques that add personality to your

ukulele playing, to make it truly your own.

Of course, playing the ukulele, like any other instrument, involves much more than just the rhythm, harmony, and melody of a song and how well you master them. As a ukulele player, you create the personality of everything you play, and you have many "personalities" to choose from! Attitude, intensity, whim, humor, surprise, speed, silence, snapping, and many other attributes are all key ingredients that can go far in creating your own personal stamp on a song or piece. This chapter covers a few techniques that will give you the facility to see how far a little personality can go!

The Muffle

Muffling is a way of "dampening" or "deadening" a sound. It's a way of controlling the notes, beat, and rhythm while you're playing. Here are a few muffle techniques for you to try.

Single Note Muffle

Play a strong, clear C note (third fret on the A string). Now raise your finger slightly so it still touches the string but so the string doesn't touch the fret. When you play it now, you will hear a dull, muffled sound. That's a single note muffle. Play that note with the finger down a few times, then lift it for the muffle. Then play 1, 2, 3, 1, 2, 3, muffling the 1 each time. Experiment with different rhythms, muffling at different times. Do you notice that you are changing the personality of the note with the changes you make?

Now play the C note and hold it so it rings clear. Cool—nice long, ringing tone. Now play it and lift your finger to a muffle just as you strike the note—a brisk, clear tone but short-lived. Note the difference.

Full Chord Muffle

Full chords can be muffled too. Make a D6 chord by placing the index finger of your left hand across all the strings at the second fret. Slightly raise your finger, but do not let it leave the string. Now mess around by trying to play this chunka-chunka rhythm pattern, which abbreviates the strum with a muffle immediately after each strum: strum, muffle, strum, muffle.

UKE TIP

There might be times while playing a solo you will want to use a strike and muffle, and other times where you think completely muffling a tone will work best. The choice is up to you and how you create your desired effect, your personality.

Muffling on the Beat

You can also muffle on an isolated beat. Try pressing the strings down on just the one beat or the three and four. Start by counting "1 and a 2 and a 3 and a 4," while muffling "and a." Or play oom-pah-pah and muffle the "pah-pahs." The idea here is to play around with muffling to create a second rhythm on top of your strumming rhythm. This can not only be great fun but can also lead to the development of your own unique playing style. It's a great doo-dad for your toolbox, so practice it and have it ready on a whim.

You can muffle from your strum hand too (we toyed with this a bit in Chapter 2 with the All Nails Strum). Use the fleshy part of your palm to "dampen" the strings as you end a downstroke. Use this muffle when you want to dampen a chord with mostly open strings.

UKE TIP

You can find interesting percussive sounds by combining the muffles of *both* hands. Just mess around with them until you hear a percussion and rhythm that you like. Then find another one.

Full-On Muffle

The New York Strum should be in every ukulele player's toolbox. This strum is actually a full-on muffle. Just hold all the strings lightly with all the fingers of the left hand and strum along to the beat of the song being played. It's great when you don't know a song but want to play along anyway—you become a "drummer" and muffle-strum along. When you get to the part you know, drop the muffle and play like mad! You have arrived. This one may have come from a jam session at the first New York Ukulele Festival in 2006.

Hammer-Ons, Pull-Offs, and Slides

These next techniques involve ways of playing notes in a more sliding, graceful way into and out of the target note. You might call the notes that come out of this technique "grace notes." They involve playing a note by the fretted hand rather than the strumming hand.

Hammer-On

For the hammer-on, let's go back to the C note on the A string. This time, let's start on the B note with your middle finger on the second fret. As you pick the B note, immediately drop your ring finger on the C note. This is called a **hammer-on**. Instead of a plain ol' C note, this one's got an "I'm here!" flavor. This particular hammer-on is a minor two interval—one half step. Hammer-ons can originate from any note below the hammered note, including, in this case, the open A string. Hammer-ons will give an extra flavor to a strummed chord too. Try hammering-on a note while strumming to break up a monotonous passage.

Pull-Off

The **pull-off** works in reverse. Hold down the C note, and as you pick it with your right hand, pull your fretting finger away, letting the A string ring. To get a good feel for what this move can do, play a steady 4/4 beat on the C chord. After you've gone through a couple of measures, pull off the C note on the third beat, snapping the A note, then let it ride through beat four, then return to the C chord for beats one and two of the next measure, and repeat the pull-off again on the third beat. This particular rhythm appears in several country songs and has a happy sound to it. Practice it, explore other combinations, and then put it in your toolbox.

UKULELE HEROES

Aaron Keim was part of the Boulder Acoustic Society and today makes ukuleles at Mya-Moe Ukuleles and performs with his wife, Nicole, as "The Quiet American." Check them out: www.quietamericanmusic.com/.

Slide

A **slide** is a variation on the hammer-on. Instead of placing a finger on the target note after picking a note lower than it, the finger on the lower note slides up the string to the target note. Slides can go backward as well. Like hammer-ons and pull-offs, slides are useful when playing melodies and solo improvisations. If you play around with them when you don't have to, you find them sneaking out of your toolbox and into your playing. That is a good thing.

Snap, Warble, and Ring

The following techniques are a way to give personality to individual notes, to really stretch them out. Try them to explore the possibilities of personality within even one tiny note.

The Snap

The **snap** can be overused, but when it's played strategically, it can be really effective. A snap is a bright, loud note that is played by pinch-snapping a string. To do the snap, take the thumb and the index finger of the strumming hand, pinch a string between them, then take the thumb a bit in front of the finger and snap the string as you pull your hand away. This move can be used at the end of a tune or significant phrase, kind of like a "button" that calls attention.

The Warble

When you hold a note while vigorously shaking the neck, the note will get a tremolo. This is a **warble**. Some players get the same effect by wriggling the finger holding the note. The effect can be very sweet. One way to perfect it is to play a single note slowly and repeatedly to learn how many personalities you can find in it. Play the note until you know it inside and out, what it likes for breakfast, and who its favorite actor is. Really get to know it. Then do the same with another note, but wait a while—you don't want to stir up any jealousies. There are few things worse than notes fighting for attention.

You can also try pulling a string faintly from side to side while holding the note. The stretching gives a warble with a slightly different character.

♫

UKE TIP

If you want to get dramatic, here's a warble to try. If you swing your ukulele overhead in the air like a bell ringing, you get a full-chord warble. The "Doppler effect" from this technique slightly changes the pitch, giving a tremolo feeling. Be careful—you can bump a friend on the noggin or smash your prized ukulele against a wall. The Australian ukulele wizard Azo Bell gets this full-chord warble by spinning his ukulele in the air, a technique that is not for everyone. This is a once-in-a-show doo-dad, easily overused. Hide it in a corner of your toolbox.

The Ring

A **harmonic** is a bell-like ring tone effect you create when the index finger is placed softly on the string above the desired fret and is pulled away just as the string is plucked by the thumb. This technique takes time and effort to learn.

When you create a harmonic on the A string at the twelfth fret, which is the middle of the string, you effectively have two "octave A" strings vibrating independently but in unison. The string vibrates in two halves. The note you hear is the octave A. A harmonic on the seventh fret introduces the fifth, the E, to the octave A.

The easiest positions to get a harmonic are the twelfth and seventh frets. You can get harmonics farther up the string if you compensate on the nut end. For example, you can get a C harmonic on the A string by holding the C note on the third fret with the left hand, while plucking the fifteenth fret with the right. Other fret locations will give harmonics on open strings, but most ukuleles don't perform them well due to the short string length.

Another way to sound a harmonic is to place the index finger of the right hand on the string directly above the desired fret and pluck the string with the thumb, pulling both away from the string as it is plucked. See the illustration. This technique allows the player to play harmonics at more locations. For example, if the player holds a B♭ note on the A string, the first fret, a harmonic can be sounded by using the index/thumb technique on the thirteenth fret. With enough practice, you can play melodies comprised completely of harmonics. It takes time, effort, and will to get this technique into the ukulele player's DNA and toolbox.

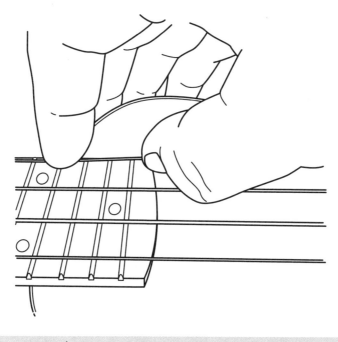

Index/thumb technique for sounding a harmonic.

A third technique for sounding harmonics is to tap the string at the fret. This works best when the ukulele has a pickup and can be amplified.

The Glissando and Two-Finger Trill

The **glissando** is sliding across a series of notes, such as playing a chord formation and moving it up the neck while strumming. It was one of the reasons I wanted to play ukulele. When I was a child, the pizza parlors featured Dixieland bands. I was intrigued by banjo players when they slid their chords. I enjoyed that sound, and I wanted to do it myself. The ukulele is one of the easiest instruments on which to get that happy sound. To enhance the glissando, add a quickened strum—the trill—presented in Chapter 2.

It's important for the glissando to be on the beat when it reaches its target. We never want to practice errors, so when learning this technique, start slow, be methodical, and keep the length of travel short. Observe the C, D7, G7, C practice illustration.

Instead of having two C notes, the two-finger C chord has two G notes. The second glissando starts on a Gm7 chord, which looks like the two-finger C chord but two frets back. We are aiming to be metrically correct in this exercise, so play slowly and count out loud. Strum the 1, 2, 3, and 4 beats of the first C chord, then strum "1 and a" on the first beat of the D♭7 chord as you move it to the D7 position, where you continue counting 2, 3, 4. Go to the next line, play the four beats of the G7 chord, and count "1 and a" while you slide the Gm7 chord to the two-finger C chord and 2, 3, 4. Start over and repeat several times. This first glissando is a one-fret, half-step move; the second one is a whole-step, two-fret move. Both distances are covered in the time of one beat that is broken into a triplet, three mini-beats in one. When comfortable with these, you will be able to play longer glissandos. This only comes with time.

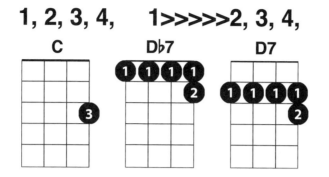

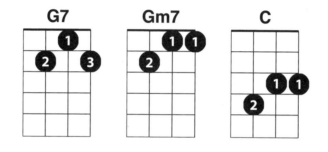

A simple glissando using both the one-finger and two-finger C chords.

Percussion

Adding a drum beat to your tune can add funk and spice. Simply tap the ukulele above the soundhole with the thumb on one of the beats of the strum. While experimenting with different strums, try throwing in a thumb tap once in a while to see what happens. Definitely worth checking out.

Here's a rarely used percussion technique I learned from the Hawaiian ukulele master Ohta-San. At the end of an exquisite jazz solo, he ran the nail of his ring finger down the fretboard from the soundhole to the nut. This made a percussive rasp, like a güiro, a serrated gourd scraped with a stick. A very cool move and unusual. Sneak it into your toolbox.

The Tritone Scramble

A friend once pointed out to me that when the **tritone** is involved, it's hard to mess up, because things are already messed up. The tritone appears in every seventh and diminished chord, and it has a disruptive, suspenseful sound.

Try it. Take the G7 triangle formation (don't worry about the G string—it's already messed up!) and play it in different spots rhythmically. When you feel the song getting to the end of a phrase, finish it off with a G7/C "two bits" home run. Takes a bit of courage, but with practice, this technique and the courage to play it will have a spot in your ukulele toolbox, and you'll be on your way to playing with total abandon.

Thanks to my friend, I discovered that I could pepper a song by goofing around all over the neck playing seventh chord formations anywhere, anytime. No matter how goofy it sounded, if I got home in time—ended the chaos with a 5–1 ending—it worked out.

UKE TIP

Remember the "shave and a haircut, two bits" exercise back in Chapter 3, when we played the root chord followed by a 5–1 ending? Keep what you learned and sensed about that 5–1 (G7/C in the key of C) in mind when thinking of the tritone: *the 5 chord goes home to the 1.* Here's a good analogy: a father tells his teenage daughter she can go out, but she needs to get home in time. She can go the movies, dinner, dancing, bowling, and a concert, and it will all be okay as long as she gets home in time.

Chapter 6

LET'S PLAY

This chapter presents a variety of songs to help you start your repertoire. Some are familiar childhood tunes that have been around for a long time, and others are more recent and unknown. Some were chosen just for fun, some to sharpen your technique. There are songs to challenge you to stretch out and explore musically too. But above all, here's my advice: start out with songs you already have in your heart and mind—they are your portal to the wide, wonderful world of song.

Learning Songs

Eventually, everyone finds his or her own best way to learn and memorize a new song. I've found a few ways to make it easier. Even songs you've sung since childhood can be elusive when you first set out to play them on the ukulele. I like to start out a new song by getting a handle on the rhythm. If I have the sheet music, I play a very simple stick rhythm, a boring but precise downstroke, counting the strokes in each measure.

Typically, a song will tend to change chords on the first beat of a measure, but chord changes can occur anywhere the composer felt like putting them. Sometimes sheet music will have "passing chords," chords that are not absolutely necessary to play the song. These are often embellishments for piano players. Just keep playing the chord that seems important until the next important chord comes along. Let your ear make the decisions.

After I've gone through a song a few times with stick rhythm and have basically gotten the idea of the song's structure, then I will start playing little chunks of it at a time. I start out with the first few bars and play it repeatedly until it sounds right. Then I walk away from the sheet music and play it to the universe, if I can remember it. I spend a lot of time walking around playing, visiting the sheet music when I get stumped.

UKE TIP

When the song "On the Beach at Waikiki" was introduced at the Panama-Pacific International Exposition in 1915, it became a huge ukulele hit. New York quickly took notice, and Tin Pan Alley, a collection of New York City music publishers, churned out Hapa Haole tunes, meaning "of white and Hawaiian ancestry." For the next two years, Hawaiian ukulele sheet music topped the sales charts.

After a while, the chunks begin to go together, and the song takes shape. I always make sure I visit the song the next day and the day after. Sometimes, once I have captured a song and made it my own, I will change the key and learn to play it in the new key. If I really like the song, I might spend years finding it on different places on the neck. Nobody says I have to do that—I just like doing it.

Once I have conquered the rhythm and basic structure of the song, I will start to pick out pieces of the melody hidden in the chords.

What Comes First—the Chicken or the Lyrics?

Sometimes the hardest song you have to learn is the one you write yourself. You write it one day, and you can't find it the next. When I was younger, I could write a couple of songs a week. Sometimes I'd get into a space where I didn't like any of the songs I once loved. Eventually, I caught on that when that feeling came on, I was on the verge of a songwriting splurge, and my dismay would blossom into anticipation.

The ukulele is an instrument, a tool. It can be taught to help you express how you feel, what you want, where you hope to be, who you love. All those heart and head and spleen juices are easily expressed in music. I hope that as you play around with the songs in this chapter, you will get ideas that drive you and your ukulele to great places.

♪

UKE TIP

Jim Beloff, one of the biggest promoters of the ukulele today, has a great series of songbooks for the ukulele. His *The Ukulele: A Visual History* is also a great resource, chock-full of the social lore and history of the uke.

Enough Already. Let's Play.

Take the time to play these songs as best you can. They are all fairly easy and have been picked to help you feel different kinds of music. Once you've had your fun with these, you should be able to scour the Internet and find thousands of tunes. Simply type the name of the song you seek with the word "chords" after it, and numerous versions of the song will be presented. I've been able to find recorded versions of just about every song on *YouTube*. Or, make something up.

UKE TIP

Buddy Craig was a marvelous guitarist who taught me a lot about playing music. Before he died, the last thing he told me was, "Forget everything I told you. Just play." It took me a couple of years before I understood what he meant. Get out of the way and let the music come through. The irony is, you can't really do that until you've mastered and absorbed the tools in your toolbox.

It Ain't Gonna' Rain No More

Traditional (1870)

It ain't gonna rain no more, no more, it ain't gonna rain no more,

How in the heck can I wash my neck if it ain't gonna rain no more?

Oh, a pea - nut sat on the rail - road track, it's
How much wood could a wood chuck chuck if a wood -
Oh, my un - cle built a chim - ney, he built
A rich man rides a taxi, a poor man rides

heart was all a flut - ter, a - round the bend came
chuck could chuck wood? If he held a saw in his
it up so high He had to tear it
a train. A bum he walks the rail - road

num - ber Ten, Toot! Toot! Pea - nut but - ter.
lit - tle paw, a ton of wood he could.
down a - gain to let the moon go by.
tracks, and he gets there just the same.

G   **D7**

You can probably find another dozen verses to this song. American poet Carl Sandburg felt the song went back as far as the 1870s. Ukulele wizard and radio personality Wendell Hall recorded a popular version of it in the 1920s. This version is in C and G7. Try it in A and E7 or G and D7. You've gotta get your feet wet on the B♭ chord sometime, so try it in B♭ and F7 too.

96

Leavin' in the Morning

Buddy Craig © 2000 Emmeline Craig

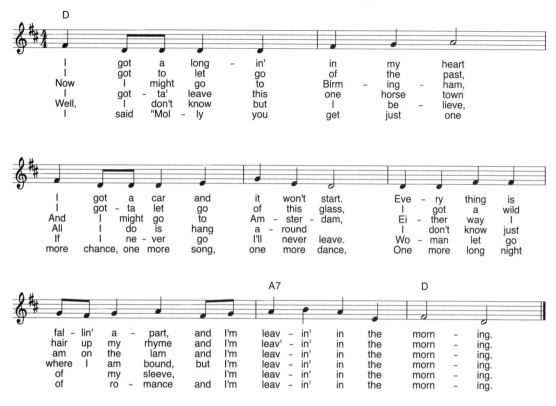

Have fun with this one—it has a country bluegrass feel.

Fog Dog Blues

© 1976 Dan Scanlan

Chorus (F) I got the standing in the fog with a wet dog - on high-way nine-ty nine blues - I'm (C7)

(F) coun-tin'- up my changes to pay the road's ex - act - in' dues. And the fog that's on the ground Oh, it's

(C7) creep-in' thru the cracks in my shoes and the numbness in my nose match-es that of my

toes, You know an-y ride I get that's good news. (F)

Verse 1 (F) Fib-ber's coiled on a tuft of weeds on a ground that's hard with frost, while I pace the pave-ment with a mind like a sal - ad that's been (C7)

(F) tossed. Dogs, I guess, just hang in there, no mat - ter what the cost; The beast will keep his own safe sleep al-though his mas-ter may be lost. (F)

Verse 2 (F) I've div-vied up my time 'tween the on-ramps and the road My bo - dy, it's the truck, my mind, the load. The (C7) (F)

(F) sleeping bag on the side of the road has been my sweet a - bode, But now I feel this grow-ing force, (C7)

and my thumb has run its course, my how this trip is get - tin' old. (F)

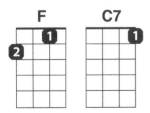

F C7

At one time I had done a lot of hitchhiking around the US, but in 1977 a VW bus failed, and I had to hitchhike home through Central California. I got stuck in the fog with my dog Fibber. As I paced back and forth to keep warm, I wrote a song, without the help of my ukulele. Then I followed a glow in the distance. It was a restaurant. It was open. I borrowed a pen and wrote the lyrics on the back of a paper placemat. I still have it. When I finally sat down with my uku-lele to put it to music, it turned out to be just two chords.

Home on the Range

Dr. Brewster Higley and Dan Kelly (1872)

Dr. Higley was a pharmacist who migrated to Kansas in 1872. He was so taken by the countryside, he wrote this song. It's simple but has some very calming chord changes from major to minor. Pay attention to the change in feeling when the chord changes from B♭ to B♭m. Really listen and try it out on other songs you play. It's a good one to have in your toolbox.

Greensleeves

Traditional (1580)

A - las my love you do me wrong to cast me off dis - cour - teous-ly and

I have loved you so long de - light - ing in your com - pa - ny

Green - sleeves was all my joy Green - sleeves was my de-light.

Green - sleeves was my heart of gold and who but La - dy Green - sleeves.

Em   **D**   **B7**

F#7   **E**   **B**

This is the oldest song we are considering—1580, according to *Wikipedia*. It's in 6/8 time, which means counting 1-2-3 twice for each measure. Notice the first measure has only one note in it—an eighth note. This measure is called a "pick-up" measure. The first downbeat—the one—is on the "-las" of "alas." Remember back in Chapter 2 when we accented the first beat? Well, the first downbeat in this song comes in the second measure (kind of like the "get set" before "go"). The ending is a little tricky. The song is in E minor—the relative, natural minor of the key of G—but the song takes a sudden plunge into E major in the last measure. Pay attention to how the sweet, somewhat mystical feeling of the minor key suddenly gets serious at the end.

Annie Laurie

William Douglas (c. 1700)

Max - well-ton braes   are   bon - nie   Where   ear - ly   fa's   the   dew;   And it's
Her   brow is   like   the   snaw drift,   Her   throat is   like   the   swan;   Her
Like dew on the   go - wan lying   Is   the   fa'   o'   her fairy - feet   And like

there   that An - nie   Lau - rie   Gie'd   me   her pro - mise   true.   Gie'd
face   it   is   the   fair - est   That   e're   the sun   shone   on;   That
winds   in sum - mer   sigh - ing   Her   voice is   low   and   sweet;   Her

me   her pro - mise   true,   Which   ne'er   for - got   will   be;   And   for   bon - nie An - nie
e're the sun shone   on,   And   dark   blue is   her   e'e,   And   for   bon - nie An - nie
voice is   low   and   sweet,   She's   a'   the world   to   me,   And   for   bon - nie An - nie

Lau - rie   I'd   lay   me doune   and   dee.
Lau - rie   I'd   lay   me doune   and   dee.
Lau - rie   I'd   lay   me doune   and   dee.

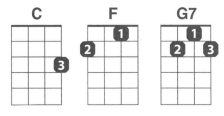

This is another old tune dating back to 1700s Scotland. The song is in 2/4 time—each measure has two quarter note beats. You can play it with four strums per measure if you want. But try it with just two strums for each measure. It will go along fine until you get to the second to last measure. Notice the G7 chord comes in not in the middle of the measure but at the very tail end. So, you have to break time a bit to catch that quick chord. It's one of the nuances that gives this tune its Scottish flair.

Don't Do Any Better

© 1973 Pat Sauer

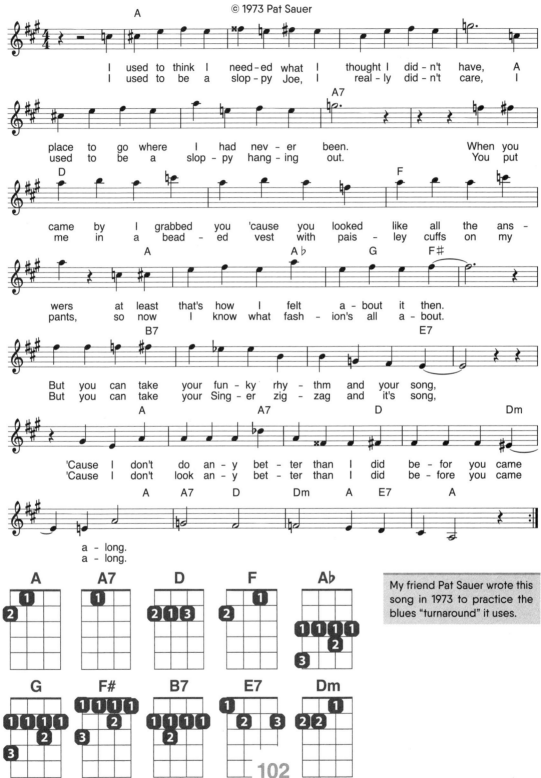

I used to think I need-ed what I thought I did-n't have, A
I used to be a slop-py Joe, I real-ly did-n't care, I

place to go where I had nev-er been. When you
used to be a slop-py hang-ing out. You put

came by I grabbed you 'cause you looked like all the ans-
me in a bead-ed vest with pais-ley cuffs on my

wers at least that's how I felt a-bout it then.
pants, so now I know what fash-ion's all a-bout.

But you can take your fun-ky rhy-thm and your song,
But you can take your Sing-er zig-zag and it's song,

'Cause I don't do an-y bet-ter than I did be-for you came
'Cause I don't look an-y bet-ter than I did be-fore you came

a - long.
a - long.

My friend Pat Sauer wrote this song in 1973 to practice the blues "turnaround" it uses.

102

Supplicant Sally

© 1993 Dan Scanlan

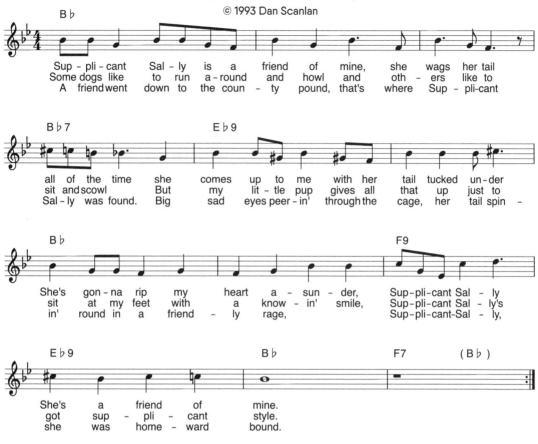

Bb

Sup - pli - cant   Sal - ly   is   a   friend   of   mine,   she   wags   her tail
Some dogs like   to   run   a - round   and   howl   and   oth - ers   like to
A   friend went   down to   the coun - ty   pound, that's   where   Sup - pli-cant

Bb7   **Eb9**

all   of   the time   she   comes   up   to   me   with her   tail   tucked   un-der
sit and scowl   But   my   lit - tle pup   gives all   that   up   just to
Sal - ly   was found. Big   sad   eyes peer - in'   through the   cage,   her   tail spin -

Bb   **F9**

She's   gon - na rip   my   heart   a - sun - der,   Sup-pli-cant Sal - ly
sit   at my feet with   a   know - in'   smile,   Sup-pli-cant Sal - ly's
in'   round in   a   friend - ly   rage,   Sup-pli-cant-Sal - ly,

Eb9   **Bb**   **F7**   **(Bb)**

She's   a   friend   of   mine.
got   sup - pli - cant   style.
she   was   home - ward   bound.

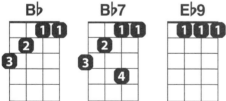

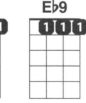

The Bb chord is usually the first chord that makes a new ukulele player think they may never be able to play. There's a way out! You can always get by by playing a Bb6 chord—simply forget about your ring finger and just use the index and middle fingers. Has a jazzy sound. Sally was an old dog friend of mine. She shows up again in the song "Good to Have You Here." This song introduces you to the 12-bar blues format. It's really a one-four-five song, but I've dressed it up for a bit of personality. Sally deserves it. (More on the blues form in Chapter 8.)

Liquid Times

© 1995 Dan Scanlan

I stand up-on this mound of years, And I can see right through your tears,
I stand be-neath a clear dark night, And see a co-met in its flight,

Feel your sad-ness and your fears and I want to walk you home. Lay you down
Its long tail of li-quid light and I want to fly you home. Shoot a star

up-on my bed, Rub out the ten-sions from your head. Re - write the words
a-cross your sky, Jump the moon as we fly, Sing that song that

that were said, I want to walk you home. To those li-quid, li-quid, li-quid, li-quid
makes you sigh, I want to fly you home.

times that course thru the pla-ces we have been Li-quid, li-quid, li-quid li-quid

times, Time and time and time and time a - gain Li-quid, li-quid, li-quid, li-quid

times.

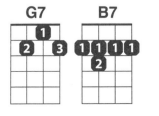

Here's a three-chord love song. I lived in a city in the nineties. There was a comet, and it was a faint streak in the sky. But when I flew south into a remote area of Mexico, the comet had a brilliant tail that swept across the sky. Love, aging, and the comet came together in this song. There's a melodic run at the end of each verse that is worth exploring.

Beautiful Dreamer

Stephen Foster (1864)

Beau-ti-ful dream-er, wake un-to me, Star-light and dew drops are wait-ing for thee

Sounds of the rude world heard in the day Lull'd by the moon light have all pass'd a - way

Beau-ti-ful dream - er queen of my song, List' while I woo thee, with soft mel-o-dy

Gone are the cares of life's bu - sy throng, Beau-ti-ful dream-er a-wake un-to me

Beau - ti - ful dream - er a - wake un - to me.

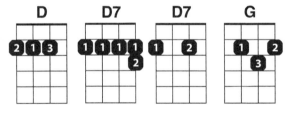

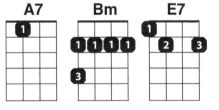

Stephen Foster was a master at creating melodies that conjured deep feelings. He pretty much created popular songwriting. The haunt of this tune is helped by its 9/8 timing. The way to handle it is to count 1-2-3 three times per measure. Some syllables—for example, "dream" in the first measure—are three beats long. Tip: When you see a quarter note with a dot, that's three beats. Each measure has the equivalent of three dotted quarter notes, which means that each measure holds nine beats. Count 'em. The D7 chord with just two strings pressed is often called the "Hawaiian D7." Try it to see if you like it.

Why Not Pretend It's True?

© 1974 Dan Scanlan

I've been hi-ding out so long for this thought to con-geal.
When we have those lit-tle spats that turn us oh, so blue,

May not be at risk at all to tell you how I feel. This
Why can't we just tip our hats, say "How do you do?" Light

love we both be-grieve it as we do the things we do, But as long as we
the wood in the stove, Smoke up the flue, As long as we

be-lieve it, why not pre-tend it's true? As long as we be-lieve it, why
be-lieve it, why not pre-tend it's true? As long as we be-lieve it, why

not pre-tend it's true? I be-lieve you love me, it's true, I love you.
not pre-tend it's true? I be-lieve you love me, it's true, I love you.

As long as we be-lieve it, why not pre-tend it's true? I be-lieve
As long as we be-lieve it, why not pre-tend it's true? I be-lieve

you love me, it's t - r - u - u - u - e, I love you.
you love me, it's t - r - u - u - u - e, I love you.

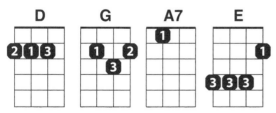

This is a basic 1-4-5 song, but in the bridge it takes advantage of the 2-5-1. If you have trouble playing the E chord, substitute an E7 chord. If you learn to play the D chord with just the ring finger, you can slide it up to the E chord without a problem and feel the "two" come into play. If you think you can do it, pretend you can.

Hymn Song

© 1973 Bruce "Utah" Phillips

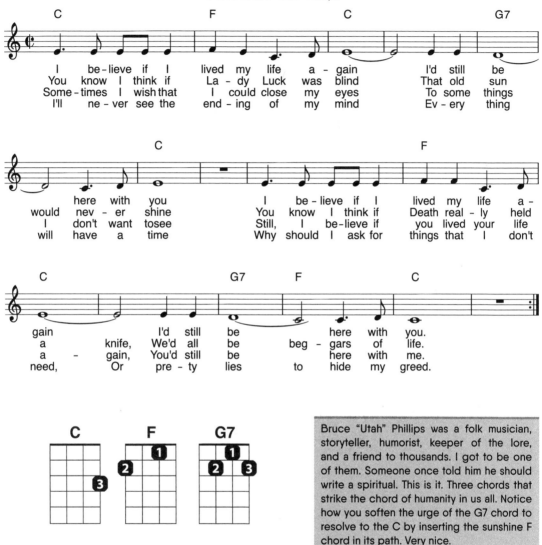

C   **F**   **C**   **G7**

I be-lieve if I lived my life a-gain I'd still be
You know I think if La-dy Luck was blind That old sun
Some-times I wish that I could close my eyes To some things
I'll ne-ver see the end-ing of my mind Ev-ery thing

C   **F**

here with you I be-lieve if I lived my life a-
would nev-er shine You know I think if Death real-ly held
I don't want to see Still, I be-lieve if you lived your life
will have a time Why should I ask for things that I don't

C   **G7**   **F**   **C**

gain I'd still be here with you.
a knife, We'd all be beg-gars of life.
a-gain, You'd still be here with me.
need, Or pre-ty lies to hide my greed.

C   **F**   **G7**

Bruce "Utah" Phillips was a folk musician, storyteller, humorist, keeper of the lore, and a friend to thousands. I got to be one of them. Someone once told him he should write a spiritual. This is it. Three chords that strike the chord of humanity in us all. Notice how you soften the urge of the G7 chord to resolve to the C by inserting the sunshine F chord in its path. Very nice.

Good to Have You Here

© 2005 Dan Scanlan

C   **Dm7**   **G7**

Doc - tor and   Sal - ly and   you on the grass,   The sun peer-ing thru the
It'sa beaut - i - ful thing, a   gal and her dogs,   A wood stove that sings,
    I am pleased to meet you and am - ble this lane, with the rocks the

Cmaj7   **C**   **Dm7**

clouds on the pass   Here creek greets the   ri - ver,   Hel - los all a -
chock full of logs   A blan - ket as   warm as the   night is
flow - ers, the wind, the   rain. In this crazy, crazed world, so ov - er - stuffed

G7   **C**   **C**   **C°**

round   It's good to have you here,   here in my town.
long,   It's good to have you here,   here in my song.   When I turn on the news,
with strife, It's good to have you here,   here in my life.

G+   **C**   **F**   **C°**   **D7**   **G7**   **C**

things don't look right.   It brings on the blues,   fears to night.   A grown up child,

F   **C**   **F**   **Am**   **Dm**   **Dm7**   **G7**

curled un - der the bed,   hopes in the morn - ing he will not be dead.

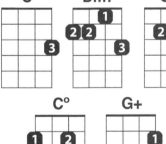

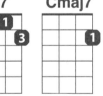

Here's Sally the dog, making her special appearance again. In a way, this is just a three-chord song, not quite a 1-4-5, but close. Technically, it's a 1-2-5. On the first go-round, instead of going home to the C, I wrote it so it goes to the Cmaj7. I did this because I wanted to maintain the "lov-ey-dovey" feeling of the song. Instead of going to an F from the C, I go to the Dm7, the two chord, which also happens to be the relative minor of F. So, in a way, I am using an F with a D note in it. It's subtle, but it gives the song a personality.

10,000 Ukuleles

Lyrics: F. Bruce, Dan Scanlan

Music: Dan Scanlan

There's a Strum Bums' performance of "10,000 Ukuleles" at the New York Ukulele Festival on *YouTube*. Watch and play along with it for practice.

Chapter 7

KEEPING ON

By now you should be well on your way to being a ukulele musician, with all the rights, privileges, joys, and expectations it can bring. In this chapter, we discuss how to keep on being a musician, growing your talent, and gathering the most joy from playing.

Play with Others

There's a lot to be said for finding a quiet place to sit, relaxing in your favorite way, and picking up your ukulele to play. Exploring to your heart's delight at leisure—working on strums, picking out melodies, toying with a tune you are writing, practicing doo-dads for your toolbox, hanging out with a chord that warms your heart—can bring a lot of joy.

Then, there's playing with others. All the work you've been doing in private suddenly needs to "fit" with what others are playing. It's a different experience altogether, as well as a different "classroom" for learning. Playing with one other person—a friend, one who might also be learning—is one kind of experience; one that hardly differs from practicing by yourself. You can easily trade what you each know and learn together.

UKULELE HEROES

Rachel Manke plays much of the American songbook and has performed on *A Prairie Home Companion* with her ukulele. Her CD, *Other Duties As Assigned*, is available through her website: http://rachelmanke.com/.

But joining a larger group of players, perhaps of people you may not know, and "jamming" with them, is another experience altogether. Playing in a group often involves customs you might not be aware of right away. In a traditional Celtic jam, players who know the songs well and play together often sit in the middle of the group. The next ring of players may not play as well, but they know the songs. Newcomers to the jam and beginners sit on the outer circle. Many non-Celtic jams work the same way, unconsciously. The bottom line is, if you are new to a jam session, keep to the outside and pay attention to how the group works. If you don't know the song that is being played, ask the person next to you, "What key is this in?" Many players will not only tell you the key, but also which chords are being played.

When you feel you have the song worked out and know where it is going, enjoy yourself. If not, keep the rhythm serenely with the "New York Strum."

Sometimes in a jam session, players will take turns soloing. Players who play together all the time will know when it's their turn to solo and will take it. In other groups, the soloists take turns going around a circle. When it comes to you, take it if you want, but if you are unsure, just turn to the next person and tell them "You take it," and pass.

UKE TIP

Most ukulele clubs warmly welcome players who are just passing through. The ukulele world is like that—friendly. Some of us used to joke that where guitar players might say, "That's not how it goes!" ukulele players would say, "Cool, is that how that goes?"

Many cities have ukulele or other music clubs that meet regularly. These groups can be large, and generally, folks simply play along. If there is a solo, it's probably the group director who takes it or someone she or he designates. Again, if you join a group, spend time quietly figuring out the group's conventions. Then, enjoy.

Form a Group

You do not have to be an accomplished, stunning ukulele player to form a musical group. Ask a couple of friends who play instruments if they'd like to form a group and get together once in a while. Duos, trios, quartets—they can be great fun and can wildly accelerate your repertoire and musical "chops." When other players are carrying a good portion of the rhythm, you can concentrate on adding a particular strum from your toolbox and then change to a different one to help give the group sound an interesting change of texture. Who knows, maybe someone will hear you playing together one day, and say, "We're having a party for my brother's birthday. Can you folks come play? We'll feed you." Food and music! Yeah!

♫

UKE TIP

Something good to know—nobody likes a boss or hog in a jam session. It's all about playing together, so respect that.

Don't Be a Jukebox, Use It!

I once heard a bass player say, "If you can't play a song exactly like it is on the radio, you shouldn't play it!" I knew a guitar player who spent months learning to play a Mississippi John Hurt song exactly the way Hurt played it, rattles and all. Those two attitudes are okay as personal preferences, but they are only two of the many avenues to enjoy playing music.

As the bandleader/teacher of a large ukulele group, one of my functions is to introduce new songs. This means I have to learn the songs and get them into my heart, brain, and fingers before I can teach them to others. I start with the sheet music, if I have it. If not, I'll find the words and chords on the Internet. I usually type the words and place the chord names over the syllable where the chord changes. Then I will sit in front of the computer and listen to a variety of versions of the song on *YouTube*. I do not intend to copy them outright; I just want to see how singers have dealt with the song in the past and what nuances they have discovered. Sometimes they change the words or phrasing. What I'm looking for is a way that works for me. When I think I've got it, I take it to the Strum Bums, my ukulele group. Sometimes, when presenting it, I realize I don't have it at all. I had it at home but not in a group setting. Another issue that confronts us is that folks remember different versions of the song. In that instance, we agree to "Strum Bum-ize" the song—i.e., make it our own; do it in a way we like.

The point here is that you do not have to be a jukebox to be a ukulele player, but it sometimes helps to check out what's in the jukebox so you can come up with your own rendition.

♫

UKE TIP

When the young and talented Jake Shimabukuro posted a *YouTube* video of himself playing a virtuosic rendition of George Harrison's "While My Guitar Gently Weeps" in 2006, he single-handedly set fire to a new blaze of interest with the ukulele—especially among young people.

Sound of Silence

I once saw Taj Mahal in a small café in Northern California. He came onto a tiny stage in a corner, sat in a chair with his guitar, and played three notes and stopped. Silence. Then he played three more notes and quit. In the silence you could hear the whole room tapping their toes in time, and he had hardly played anything. Years before, I was working on a car for a friend who was a blues drummer. I crawled out from under the car and went with him into his house to grab a drink. As we passed through his living room, he quickly sat and played one or two measures on the drums, got up, and continued walking. "That's the blues," he said, "it's always going on. You just join it."

I believe that in music, silence is not the absence of sound, it's the pattern of sound. When Taj Mahal played a few notes and stopped, he didn't stop the rhythm. He kept counting, and when he finally played another note it was right on the beat. The music did not stop.

An exercise that can help you understand this is to play a song you know well, perhaps singing the song in your head. Then, at some moment, stop playing but keep the song going in your head, and when it feels right, come back into the song continuing with your strum. In other words, try stopping the strum without stopping the song. This will help you know your music from the inside out. If you do it often enough, the technique will find a place in your toolbox.

Record Yourself

Just about everybody these days has an audio recorder in their pocket on the phone. Record yourself playing a chord sequence, say, C, F, G7, and C again. Play it a few times metrically correct, one bar each chord. Put it on repeat, then play and strum along with it. Then play the notes in the C scale any way you wish, but come back to the C note every time the sequence reaches the end of four bars. Try starting your solo from a different note each time and see where it leads. The thing to remember is to "get home in time"! If you find you can't play along with the recording, maybe you missed a beat. Mess with it 'til you get it right.

Get Into Ukulele Lore

The ukulele has a wonderful history and vast repository of lore. As a player, you are now part of it.

UKE TIP

Ardent ukulele players tend to relish the instrument's history and lore. In the 130 years of its existence, the ukulele enjoyed four "waves" of popularity. The first came in 1915, when the Panama-Pacific International Exposition in San Francisco featured Hawaiians in coconut bras and grass skirts dancing to the ukulele. A second wave came during World War II when soldiers took their ukuleles onto the battlefield. A third wave came in the late forties when Arthur Godfrey, a famous broadcaster, played it on his radio program and even lent his name to the little plastic ukuleles being made at the time. A fourth wave came with the Internet: by the end of the nineties, the ukulele was all over the web, with enthusiasts and players growing connections daily in cyberspace.

Teach Someone

I'm lucky to be the oldest of nine kids. Not only did I learn their names one at a time, but I got to teach them all kinds of things—how to climb to the upper cabinets where the candy is, how to tie their shoes, how to ride a bike, how to play "Walk Right In." When I taught one of my brothers to play Ping-Pong, I suddenly played better myself. I know for a fact that teaching what you know about the ukulele to others will increase your own command of the instrument and your musicality and will lessen your karmic debt.

Just Play

I read that a woman once said to Louis Armstrong, "I heard you play that song before, but you didn't play it like that." Satchmo is reputed to have answered, "I've got to be entertained too." Here's the moral of that story: enjoy yourself; just play.

Chapter 8

CHORDS

This chapter is your library of chords. Explore them, practice them, and make them your own. There are 180 chords listed here by root name. I've also included common chord sequences and patterns in music, as well as some ways that chords are manipulated in different styles of music. The idea is to help you get the building blocks to anticipate patterns in songs so you can pick them up easily and the basics to help you start to write your own songs.

The Chord Collection

Your main chord collection is shown on the following pages. Each image shows a collection based on a root note.

The first row shows the major, major seventh, dominant seventh, sixth, and ninth chords based on the tonic. The next row shows the minor chords and the two augmented chords based on the tonic. The last row illustrates the first diminished chord (it repeats every third fret), a major chord with a "suspended" fourth, the augmented and diminished fifths, the major chord with an added ninth, and the next inversion of the major chord on the neck.

Note that some chord formations have two names, depending on the context in which they are used. For example, a G9 chord is identical to a Dm6 chord. A G9 chord can take the place of a G7 or G chord, while the Dm6 might take the place of a Dm chord. You might notice that D and G are the four and five of one another. Every minor sixth chord has a look-alike, sound-alike ninth chord in a different key. A similar relationship exists between minor sevenths and sixths. The ukulele itself is tuned to a C6 chord or, if you wish, an Am7 chord. So, too, exists the look-alike of a ninth chord with a minor sixth chord, as in A9 and Fm6.

One last note before entering the chord charts. A diminished chord can be named for any note in it. A diminished chord is a dominant seventh chord with every note in it flattened except the tonic. In a simple twist of mathematical fate, it turns out that all four notes can act as a tonic. Again, the name used depends on where it is used and which of the notes relates to the melody.

I have chosen to name certain chord groups according to their relative popularity. Thus, I called a group E♭ rather than D♯, another B♭ instead of A♯, C♯ rather than D♭, and F♯ instead of G♭. But they can be called by either name. Again, it depends on the context.

Here's why I brought all this up: don't let it confuse you. It's not you, it's just how it is.

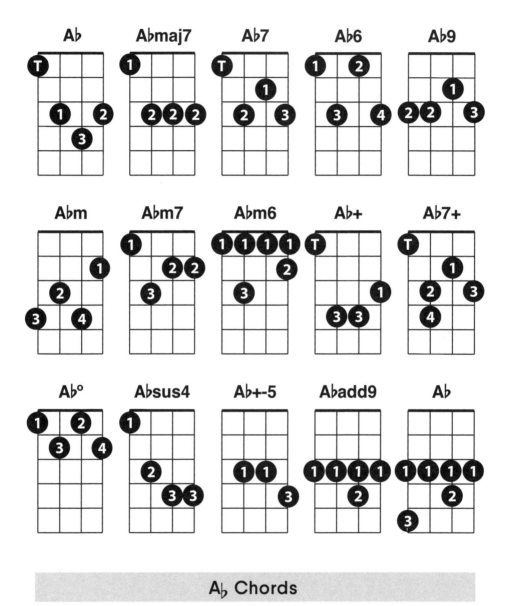

Ab Chords

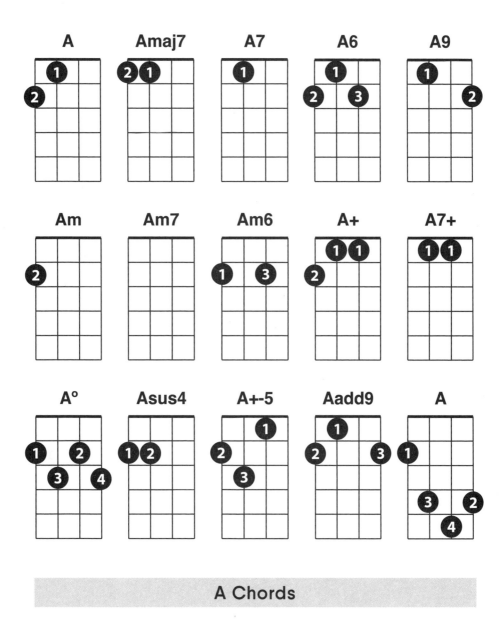

A Chords

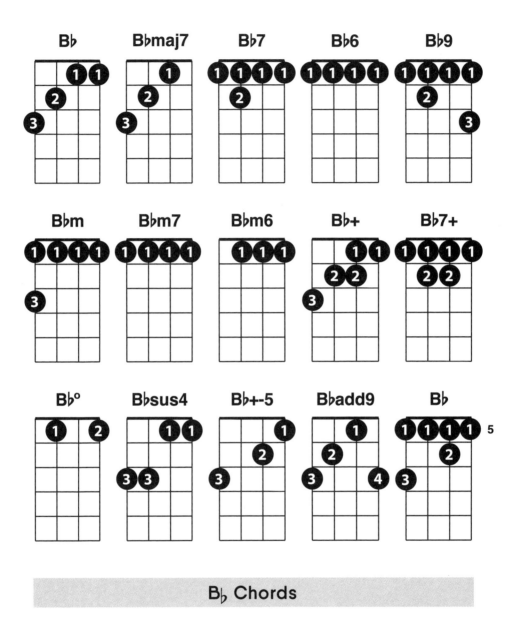

Bb Chords

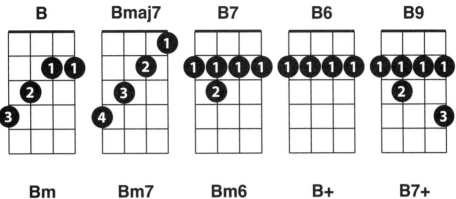

B   Bmaj7   B7   B6   B9

Bm   Bm7   Bm6   B+   B7+

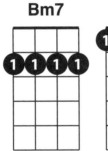

Bº   Bsus4   B+-5   Badd9   B

B Chords

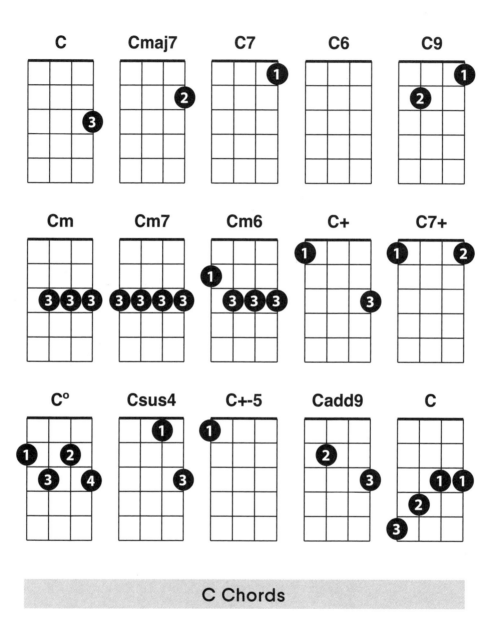

C Chords

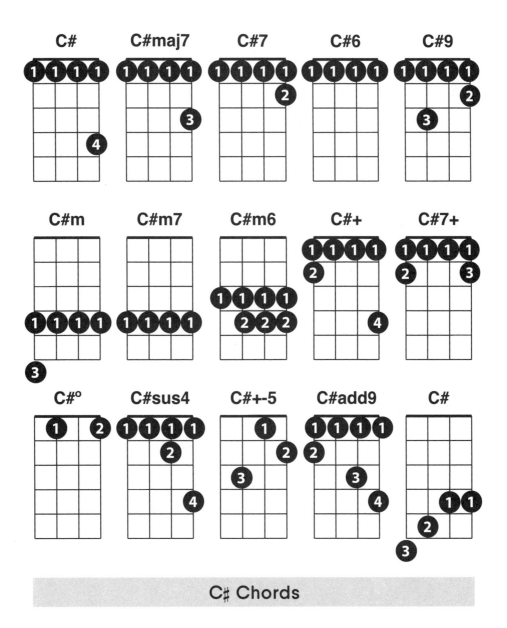

C# Chords

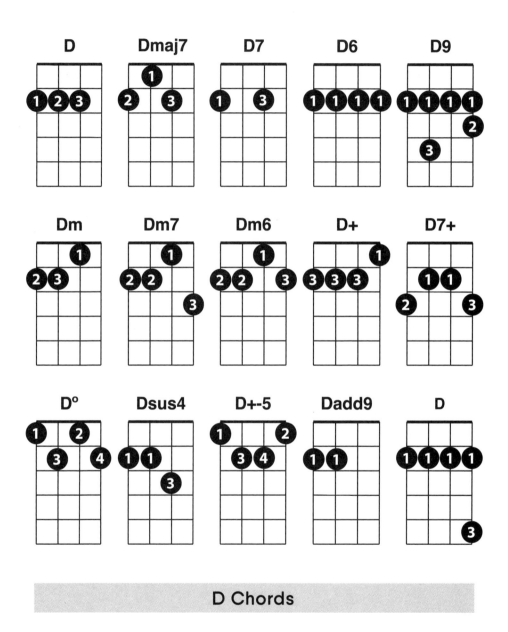

D Chords

128

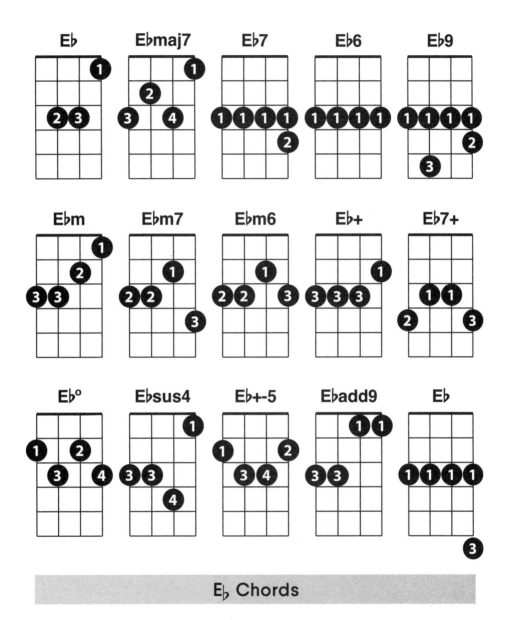

E♭ Chords

129

E   **Emaj7**   **E7**   **E6**   **E9**

Em   **Em7**   **Em6**   **E+**   **E7+**

E°   **Esus4**   **E+-5**   **Eadd9**   **E**

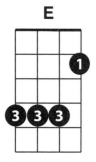
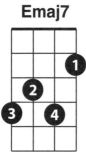
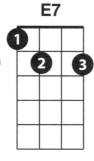
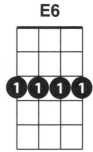
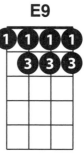
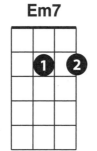
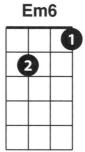
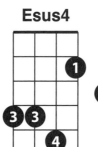
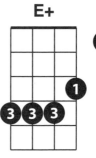

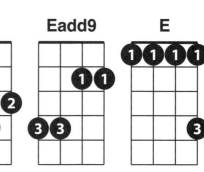

E Chords

130

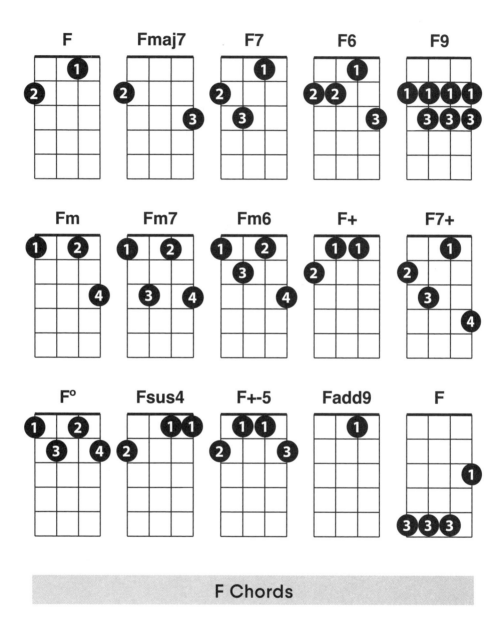

F Chords

131

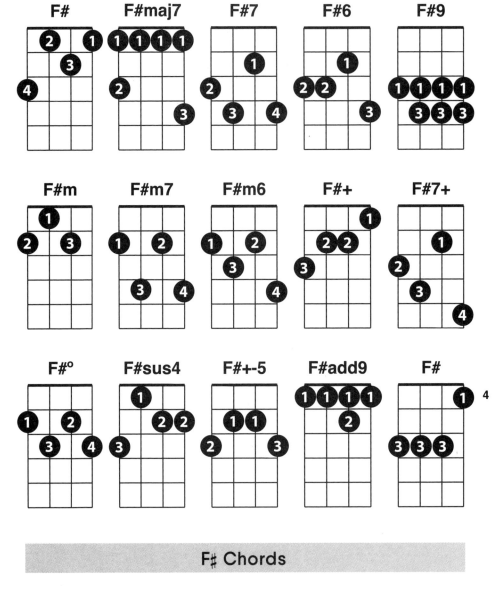

F# Chords

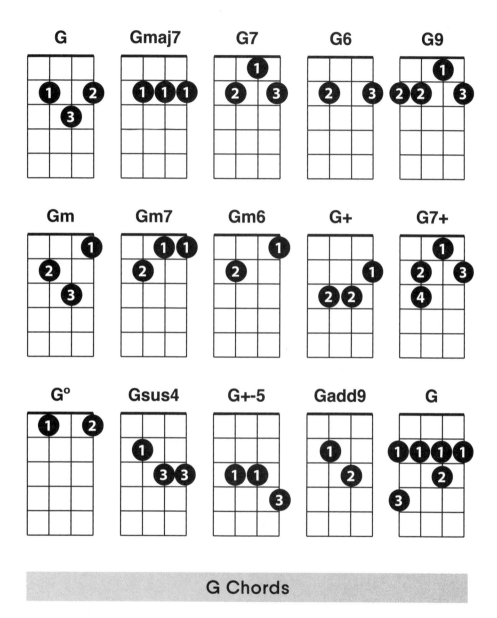

G Chords

Changing Keys

Sometimes you may need to change the key of a song on a whim to fit your voice or to play along with someone who likes a different key. When you do change the key, the notes of the melody change, and so do the chords. The notes and chords must, though, keep the same place as they did in the previous key. Changing the key *before* you play the song is called **transposing**. Changing the key *during* a song requires **modulation**, a movement to make it flow. The most common way to modulate on the fly to a new key (or to restart a song when you forget where you are!) is to go to the two chord of the key you want, then to the five chord, and finally to the new tonic chord, the one. This is the **two-five-one** turnaround we have mentioned before. After modulation or whenever you want to change the key, you must transpose. The transposition chart shows which chords go where with which key. It's probably a good idea to memorize the common chords (the one, two, three, four, five, and six) for the most common keys—namely, C, F, G, D, A, E, and B♭.

Find the key in column 1 of the song you wish to change to a new key. That row contains the chord root names of the most likely chords used in that key. To play in the new key, use the new likely chords in the new key's row. The bottom of the table shows the most common use of the chords shown in that column.

Common Chord Patterns

As we saw in Chapter 6, there are some chord patterns that repeatedly appear in music, like the one-five-one chord pattern and the one-four-one-five-one pattern. Both of these are widely used in music throughout the world. (Some musicians contend that the one, four, and five chords are all you really need to get by.) Let's take a look at some other common ones—they're going to be worth having in your toolbox.

TRANSPOSITION CHART						
1	**2**	**3**	**4**	**5**	**6**	**7**
A♭	B♭	C	D♭	E♭	F	G°
A	B	C♯	D	E	F♯	G♯°
B♭	C	D	E♭	F	G	A°
B	C♯	D♯	E	F♯	G♯	A♯°
C	D	E	F	G	A	B°
C	D♯	F	F♯	G♯	A♯	C°
D	E	F♯	G	A	B	C♯°
E♭	F	G	A♭	B♭	C	D°
E	F♯	G♯	A	B	C♯	D♯°
F	G	A	B♭	C	D	E♯°
F♯	G♯	A♯	B	C♯	D♯	F♯°
G	A	B	C	D	E	F♯°
major maj7 7, 6, 9	7 m m7	7 m m7	major 9	major 7, 9 aug	7 m m7	dim

UKE TIP

Remember how we said in Chapter 5 that the 5 chord always wants to "go home" to the 1 chord? A friend once said music is everything that happens in between. All Western music, he explained, is "a fight between the one and the five—music is just the way to get to the five so you can get back to the one." Pretty simple, but sometimes it's best to keep it simple, maestro.

Ice Cream Chords

No one knows exactly why, but the chord sequence one-six-four-five has been called the "Ice Cream Chords" or the "Blue Moon Chords." I was introduced to this sequence when learning the song "26 Miles Across the Sea," playing C, Am, F, and G7, in that order. "Stand by Me," "Earth Angel," "Heart and Soul," and many other songs use this pattern. Try playing the sequence in several keys (use the transposition chart), and you may start hearing it everywhere.

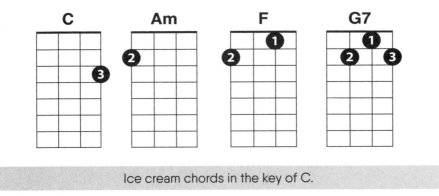

Ice cream chords in the key of C.

136

Common Chord Sequences

Songwriters have made great music by using simple repetition of simple chords in a simple sequence. Let's take a look at some of the sequences you might find useful in your quest to make great music.

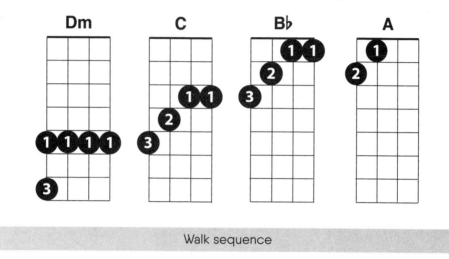

Walk sequence

A version of this walk-down was made famous in the surf guitar tune "Walk, Don't Run." It can be used to start off a song or add a bit of flavor randomly. I wrote a sentimental song when my mother died and later realized I had used this sequence but in a different rhythmic structure. It's a good one to have in your toolbox.

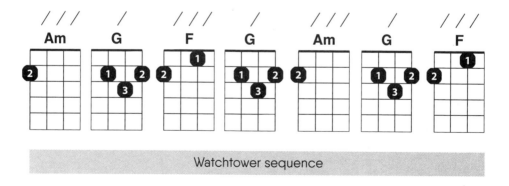

Watchtower sequence

This is the chord structure used in one of the most famous rock jam tunes, Bob Dylan's "All Along the Watchtower." It basically rocks back and forth between an Am chord and F, with a single beat on the G chord on every fourth beat, as indicated by the slashes. This riff, and others like it, serves as a backdrop for improvising. It shows that a simple riff, well executed, can be powerful music.

Blues Chords

Twelve-bar blues is a favorite form of the blues throughout the world. Thousands of songs use the form, and once a player understands it, blues tunes come easily. It is remarkable how many variations are possible on this otherwise rigid structure. Here's the fundamental form:

12-BAR BLUES											
I	I	I	I	IV	IV	I	I	V	IV	I	V
C	C	C	C	F	F	C	C	G	F	C	G
A7	A7	A7	A7	D7	D7	A7	A7	E7	D7	A7	E7
C	C	C	C7	F	F	C	C	G7	F	C	G7
B♭6	B♭6	B♭6	B♭7	E♭9	E♭9	B♭6	B♭6	F9	E♭9	B♭6	F#9/F9
Am	Am	Am	Am	Dm	Dm	Am	Am	Em	Dm	Am	Dm

The top row shows where the one, four, and five chords are played. Each rectangle represents one 4-beat measure. The second row shows the basic chords in the key of C. The third row not only shows the chords in the key of A but also demonstrates that sometimes players like to play the whole thing in seventh chords. The next row shows the blues in C again, but with some changes often made, such as adding the seventh in the fourth measure. The B♭ row shows how sixths and ninths can be used in a blues tune, as well as the use of a "stretch five" in the twelfth measure. The final row illustrates that the minor blues uses the same structure but with minor chords.

8-BAR BLUES							
I	V	IV	IV	I	V	I/IV	I/V
A7	E7	D7	D7	A7	E7	A7/D7	A7/E7

The top row shows which chords are played at which time. Notice that even though there are fewer measures, there are more changes in the 8-bar blues. The bottom row gives you something to play right now—8-bar blues in A.

THE BLUES TURNAROUND			
I/I7	IV.iv	I/V7	I
C/C7	F/Fm	C/G7	C
I/I7	IV.iv	I/♯V7/V7	I
A/A7	D/Dm	A/F7/E7	A

This turnaround can be played in several ways. The first and second rows show one way, where each chord gets two beats and in the final measure has just one beat. The next two rows show the turnaround where the final two measures use a "stretch five" to "walk-down" to the final beat. It is also possible to hold the stretch five for two beats, then play the five and the one for two beats. Try it both ways. Some players will end a tune with this turnaround and stop it to milk it for all it's worth.

The Circle of Fifths

As we have seen, the five is the dominant note in a scale or the dominant chord in a song. Regardless of which key a song is in, the five drives the song or melody home to the tonic chord or note. Consider this: the five is the one to somebody. It has a five too. You could say that every "one" has a "five of a five"! Holy mackerel! This could drive us in a circle! And it does. The outer ring shows the fives of all twelve keys.

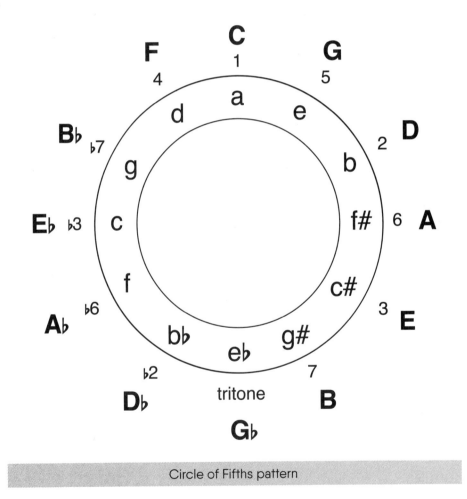

Circle of Fifths pattern

The outer ring has the chord or note name, beginning with the C note. The fifth of C is G, which is clockwise. Its fifth is clockwise as well, and so on. Going in the other direction, the note counterclockwise to C is F, its fourth. Continuing in the same direction is B♭, the fourth of F. So, the fourths run counterclockwise, and the fifths clockwise. The numbers specify where in the scale of C the note or chord is located. The lowercase letters in the inner circle are the relative minors of each key.

Many songs use some part of the Circle of Fifths. "Five Foot Two, Eyes of Blue," which is a song that ukulele players must be able to play (unofficial but stringent law), follows the Circle to a tee: "(C) Five foot two, (E7) Eyes of blue, But (A7) Oh, what those five feet could do, has (D7) anybody (G7) seen my (C) gal?" Looking quickly at the Circle, you see the song follows the Circle exactly: 1-3-6-2-5-1 or, in the key of C: C-E-A-D-G-C. Competent musicians may call out a song as, "Circle, in C."

Notice that the three chords most used in songs—the 1, 4, and 5—are all at the top. Thousands of songs don't go any further than this around the Circle.

Two, Five, One

The next most frequently used chunk of the Circle is the 2-5-1. In the case of C, this is D, G, C, or Dm7, G7, C; or D9, G9, C6. Country songs use it: "…(2) How's about cookin' (5) somethin' up with (1) me?" And jazz tunes: "(1) Gotta get my (2) old tux- (5)-edo (1) pressed." I used this sequence in my song "Good to Have You Here": "(1) Doctor and Sally, and (2) you on the grass, the (5) sun peering through the (1) clouds on the pass." There were some "fancy" chords—C, Dm7, G7, Cmaj7—but it was still 1-2-5-1.

As we have seen earlier, the 2-5-1 is often used to change key in a song by using the two chords of the key you want to play. That will lead to the five and from there to the new key.

Another function of the 2-5-1: if you get lost in a song or can't remember where you are, you can always sneak back to the beginning with a 2-5-1.

UKE TIP

I once spent a week at a peace camp. People came from all over the world. One night I was asked to play "Stardust" as folks walked to the evening wrap-up. Someone was talking to me as I played and walked. Suddenly, I didn't know where I was in the song. I just went blank. Later I was jamming with a saxophone player from Paris. I told him what had happened. He laughed and said, "2-5-1!"

One benefit of knowing the Circle of Fifths is that if you know which chord is being played at the moment, you have a good shot at knowing what the next chord will be, simply because every chord is the five of something and needs to go home to it. Sure, there are exceptions, lots of them, but when they come around, you may hear them as exceptions.

We've said that the simplest songs have two chords, the one and the five. But if you listen to a lot of Celtic and bluegrass music you will hear two-chord songs that are one and flat-seven, such as "Orange Blossom Special" and "Old Joe Clark": "(1) Fare thee well, Old Joe Clark, fare thee well I (♭7) say. (1) Fare thee well, Old Joe Clark, (♭7) I'm a-going a-(1)way." Check out the Circle again. Notice that the flat seven (B♭, in the key of C) is the four of the four of C. Weird. It strikes me that since the relative minor of B♭ is Gm, there has to be a taste of G in the chord. And there is. B♭ and G7 chords each have F and D notes in them. One could make the case that playing a tune that rocks back and forth between C and B♭ is just a wacky C and G7 with a back-porch sensibility.

Traditionally, the Circle of Fifths is illustrated with C at the top. The key of C has only natural tones and no "accidentals," no black keys simplifying the presentation. Also, all the note names on the right-hand side have sharps in their scales, starting with one sharp in G, two in D, three in A, and so on. All the flat keys are on the left, F having one flat, B♭ two, E♭ three, and so on.

If you could move the numbers around so that the one landed on a differ-ent tone—G, for example—then C would be the four, D the five, A the two, E the six, and B the three. The relationship stays the same; only the names (and actual tones) have changed. Fact is, if you know the Circle, you can jump in anywhere and play it all the way home. You'll never regret learning it.

The Circle on the Neck

Just as a certain chord is apt to follow a particular chord, on the ukulele neck, certain chord shapes follow others.

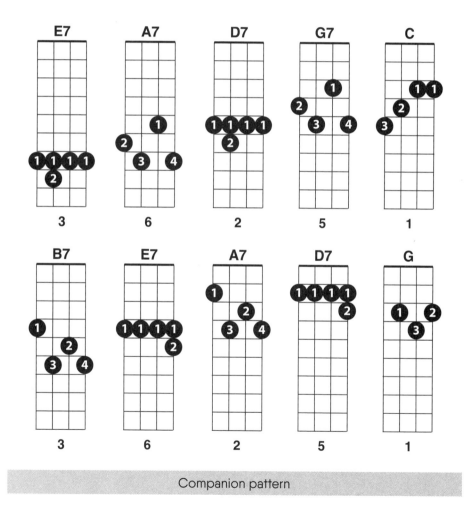

Companion pattern

If you choose to play farther up the neck, you will notice that there are companion chord shapes that follow one another. In the first row of chords, a set of companion chord shapes are shown in the key of C. A different set of chord shapes do the same thing in the lower row of chords.

Play a one-finger C chord, then slide the shape shown in the first diagram in the top row of the illustration from the beginning of the fretboard to the seventh fret, making a glissando effect. Strum a measure, then work your way back to the second position C chord. Those chords rocking back and forth follow the Circle of Fifths. Try switching to other keys. For example, starting with an A chord, slide to the fourth fret and follow the same pattern back to A. In time, you might find it fun to follow the pattern but using substitute chords, like ninths and major sevenths. No one gets hurt if you experiment.

Sliding Chords

Sometimes it's fun to dress up a song with a two-note sliding chord sequence. These walk-downs or walk-ups are often used in country and Hawaiian music. They are fun to find on your own. Two common ones are illustrated.

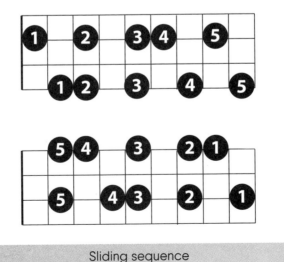

Sliding sequence

The top row shows sliding chords ascending in the key of F. The numbers denote the pairs of notes that are played together, not the finger that is used. The second row descends in the key of C.

I use the index and middle fingers for the slanted pairs and the middle and ring fingers on the pairs that are on the same fret. You can stop on the C (pair number four) or continue to pair five, then back to pair four. Country-western players like to start on pair two and walk it down to the C (pair four). Sometimes they throw a chromatic scale walk-down between pair two and three. Try picking the two-note chords in triplets, picking the lower string, upper, then lower, and move to the next position and repeat. Try gliding a finger up into position from the fret next to it for a bit of cow-patty ambiance as you finish a run.

Appendix A

GLOSSARY

Here you'll find definitions of the terms used in this book—and some others that you may encounter as you pursue your ukulele escapade.

Amen Chord

The four chord in a song. Named for the "Ah-h-h-h" of "Amen."

Augmented

Raised half a tone, or one fret; sharpened. In a chord, the fifth note is raised a half step to create an augmented chord, an added mellow anticipation. When a whole five chord is notched up a half step, some musicians call it a "stretch five." Once played, it drops back to the five and then back to the one, the root tone (tonic).

Banjo-Uke

A ukulele constructed with a banjo-style body rather than a guitar-style body. Invented in the 1920s. Some are as small as six inches in diameter. Some have open backs; others have an additional back that acts as a resonator. Also called banjo-lele and uke-banjo.

Barre Chord

A chord in which all the strings are stopped on one fret by the index finger. The other fingers make the remainder of the chord as though the index finger were the nut. For example, by making a barre with the finger on the first fret, then pressing the A string on the fourth fret, a C♯ chord sounds. In effect, the nut has moved up a fret. See *capo* for a similar result.

Capo

A device to shorten the strings on a string instrument to make playing in some keys easier. Capos made for ukuleles usually consist of a steel rod the width of the neck inside plastic tubing, and are held in place with an elastic band. Example: by placing a capo on the third fret and playing a song using the C chords, the actual key will be that of E♭. The other way to do this is to barre the third fret with the index finger and use the other fingers to play the chords. Either way, the nut has been effectively "moved."

Circle of Fifths

All twelve tones of the chromatic scale are arranged in a circle so that each tone sits between its five and its four. The circle is normally shown with the C note at the top, the keys with sharp notes in their scale are to the right, and the keys with flats in their scale are to the left.

Diminished

Lowered, or flattened, by half a note or one fret. A diminished chord is a dominant flat seventh chord with all the notes flattened except the root note. Diminished chords have four possible names—thus, there are only three diminished chords before they repeat themselves going up the neck. When a two, three, or six note is flattened, it is called *minor*, rather than *diminished*, a word used for the one, four, five, and octave notes and chords.

Dominant

The fifth note in a scale or the fifth chord in a key. The five note above the octave is the second harmonic of any note. (The octave is the first harmonic.) The five chord usually carries the tension in a song and creates the need to "go home," i.e., return to the root tone. The dominant chord often contains a flatted seventh note in addition to the one, three, and five notes. This creates a tritone between the seventh and third notes in the chord, creating additional tension.

Drone

A note, usually an open string, that sounds throughout a passage without change. The G string can be left open when playing in the key of C or G, giving an old-time banjo sound.

Felt Pick

A thick, teardrop- or pear-shaped slab of heavy felt used to play melodies on the ukulele. Rarely used in modern times except by jazz soloists. Most players use their unadorned fingers to play, although using guitar picks is not uncommon.

First Position Chord

The simplest form of a chord that is played as close to the nut as possible. Other chords with the same name and tones are called inversions, or second, third, or fourth position chords.

Flat

Opposite of sharp. Out of tune, if referring to a string or pitch; a note between two natural notes, if referring to note names. A black key to the left of a white key on the piano. An E♭ is a note; a flat E is a note that's not quite an E and could easily be called a sharp E♭!

Geometry

In this book, the pattern and location of notes and intervals in scales, sequences of chords in songs, and the placement of fingers on the fretboard when playing.

Glissando

The act of strumming a chord while sliding it to a new position.

Harmonic

Harmonics are tones that are higher in frequency than the root tone but are heard (with lower volume) along with the root tone. The octave is the first harmonic, the fifth above the octave is the second harmonic, and so on. The relative volumes of harmonics help listeners to determine whether an instrument is a ukulele, guitar, mandolin, saxophone, etc. Harmonics are also clear, bell-like tones that are heard when strings are lightly touched at certain fret positions and the string is allowed to vibrate strongly from both ends with a common center.

Harmony

The pleasing sound of two or more tones played together, as in chords.

Home

The tonic chord or note, the one, the root, the key tone of a song in melody and harmony, or the one beat of the rhythm. When a song "goes home," there is a sensation of resolution and completion.

Interval

The distance between two tones. For example, the distance between C and G is a fifth, called a "perfect fifth" by classicists. C to F is a perfect fourth. The interval between F and C, however, is a perfect fifth, since there are more steps to take to get from F to C than there are to get from C to F. From C to E is considered a major third, but from C to E♭ is called a minor third. Some people can identify intervals easier than pitches.

Inversion

The form a chord can take. For example, the first inversion of a C chord is one finger on the third fret of the A string. The second inversion is a B♭ pattern that starts on the third fret of the A string and continues across the other three strings, making the same notes but on different strings. On some inversions, the notes will be octaves of themselves, being played farther up the neck.

Leading Tone

The seventh note in the scale, leading to the octave. It has a feeling of needing to complete. There are other conditions sometimes referred to as leading tones. For example, a G7 chord can be said to have two leading tones—the B, which is the leading tone in the C scale, leading to C, and the F, which will lead to the E tone of the C chord when it is played. Both the B and F lead to a note of the C chord.

Major

A chord based on one, three, and five, or a stack of major thirds (three is the third of one, and five is the third of three). In a C chord, C, E, and G comprise the stack of thirds (E is the third note from C, and G the third from E). Also refers to unflattened notes of the scale.

Mediant

The third note in a scale. Sometimes flattened to make a minor chord.

Minor

A chord with a flattened three. For example, a C chord is C, E, and G, but a C minor chord is C, E♭, and G. Minor chords have a mysterious or mellow feeling to them. Minor also describes a flat two or six note in a scale, as well as the three.

Noodling

The act of unconsciously playing a favorite song segment, chord sequence, doo-dad, or melody while trying to figure out what to play.

Octave

The eighth note in a scale, having the same name as the tonic. It is the first harmonic of any note.

Pane

A Hawaiian word, pronounced *pah-nay*, that is a 2-5-1 chord sequence that leads into a traditional Hawaiian song. It can also mean jamming or improvising.

Passing Chord

A chord that adds flavor to a chord sequence. It need not be played. For example, a song can go from C to G7, or it could go from C to Dm7 to G7, or C to G♯7 to G7. In this example, Dm7 and G♯7 could be considered passing chords. Some songs do rely on the interim chord; others don't. It's up to the musician to decide what works and feels right.

Pulsing

An additional rhythmic pattern, usually added to the underlying beat by regularly dampening the strings while strumming. Pulses can also be generated with the strumming hand by varying the speed and force of the strum rhythmically. The beat goes on, but the pulses rise and fall.

Root

The note on which a chord is based, also called the tonic or one. The root of a C major chord is C.

Sharp

Opposite of flat. Out of tune, if referring to a string or pitch; a note between two natural notes, if referring to note names. A black key to the right of a white key on the piano. An F♯ is a note; a sharp F is an out-of-tune note that's higher in tone than an F and could easily be called a flat F♯!

Stretch Five

A five chord raised one fret, sometimes used to end a song by adding a bit of flair to the final five chord, which follows it before going home to the one.

Subdominant

The fourth note in a scale or chord in a key. A whole note below the five note and chord. Sometimes called the "sunshine chord" or the "Amen chord."

Submediant

The sixth note in the scale. The sixth is also home of the relative minor key of the tonic. For example, A is the sixth note in the scale of C, and an A minor scale has exactly the same notes as the C scale (all the white keys of the piano), but the scale starts and ends with A notes. A common way to enter the Circle of Fifths is to "walk-down" the tonic to the submediant—for example, C to A—then to "go home" by way of the Circle of Fifths.

Sunshine Chord

One of the nicknames of the four chord.

Supertonic

The second note in the scale. Literally, above the tonic.

Suspended

A fourth added to a major chord—for example, an F added to a C major chord. Gives the chord a sweet feeling of just hanging out.

Tonic

The note on which a scale or chord is based. The one note of a scale or key note of a song. Sometimes called the root or home.

Tritone

An interval of three whole tones. Called "the Devil's tone" in the Middle Ages, because it has a very dissonant sound. Falls between the four and the five (the subdominant and dominant) in the scale. When it is used in the minor pentatonic scale, it is called the blue note.

Appendix B

RESOURCES

In this appendix, you'll find information you need to help get connected to the ukulele scene and to continue building your knowledge and skills. Listed are prominent ukulele performers and the best teachers in the community, different publications and media devoted to the ukulele, and sites for ukulele festivals and clubs (including some advice on forming one on your own). There's also a bit of information on ukulele manufacturers to help you find a good instrument. So go forth and find your own ukulele community—they're waiting for you.

Cyber Connections: Players and Teachers

One of the biggest reasons the ukulele is enjoying a resurgence in popularity? The Internet. The Internet allowed ukulele players across the world to find each other, and from there new clubs and festivals were born. Guitar makers started making ukuleles again, as did numerous individual luthiers.

The number of ukulele performers who taught also rose. Today, thousands of ukulele performers and teachers are working in practically every corner of the world. Here are some of the best (and my favorites).

https://jameshillmusic.com
Not only a world-class stunning player, James Hill of Canada also teaches and certifies ukulele teachers in this extensive course.

http://fountainofuke.blogspot.com
Lil' Rev of Wisconsin is a multi-instrumentalist who features the ukulele in his teaching and performances, and is steeped in Tin Pan Alley, folk, and Jewish music.

www.ukulele.org
One of the oldest ukulele sites, the Ukulele Hall of Fame Museum in Cranston, Rhode Island, pays homage to players of old and maintains a collection of historically significant ukuleles.

www.manitobahal.com
Manitoba Hal, now of Nova Scotia, is a wonderful player of blues on the ukulele.

www.victoriavox.com
Victoria Vox of California is a prolific songwriter, ukulele player, and recording artist.

www.petermossuke.com
Peter Moss of England travels the world teaching his style of high-energy ukulele.

www.coolhanduke.com

This is the author's site, *Cool Hand Uke's Lava Tube*, one of the oldest ukulele sites on the Internet.

www.danijoymusic.com

Dani Joy, of Grass Valley, California, is a ukulele teacher, workshop presenter, and leader of a ukulele-based combo.

www.keokikahumoku.com

Keoki Kahumoku is the son of slack key guitarist George Kahumoku Jr. He introduced me to sliding chords on the ukulele.

www.playukulelebyear.com

Jim D'Ville is an animated workshop presenter who teaches how to play ukulele by ear.

www.fleamarketmusic.com

Jim and Liz Beloff created this website, which features a bulletin board and other services. They have published a variety of songbooks for the ukulele.

www.ukalady.com

Michelle Kiba is the Ukulele Lady of the Santa Cruz, California, area, and is a prolific workshop presenter.

www.kevincarroll.net

Kevin Carroll is a ukulele teacher and performer in Austin, Texas, and a leader of a youth "ukestra."

http://geraldross.com

Gerald Ross is an accomplished lap steel and ukulele performer and workshop presenter.

Ukulele Publications and Media

Ukulele publications are also thriving. Here are some notable sources of news and media resources for the ukulele enthusiast.

https://kamuke.com
Australian magazine devoted to ukulele playing, created by ukulele performer Cameron Murray.

www.ukulelemag.com
An online magazine with player profiles, bits of history, and other things "ukulele."

www.ukuleleyes.com
Online instructions, including an archive of older lessons.

www.doctoruke.com/songs.html
This site features words and chords to more than 2,000 songs for the ukulele.

Ukulele Festivals

These days, ukulele festivals are everywhere. Ukulele performances and workshops are even showing up in folk and world music festivals. Here I list some of my favorites. A quick search engine hunt for ukulele festivals will easily yield hundreds more.

www.ukulelefestivalhawaii.org/en/
The granddaddy of ukulele festivals, this festival has been running nearly half a century in Honolulu on the first week of August every year. I have been very fortunate to perform at this wonderful event several times.

http://ukulelefestivalnorcal.org/aboutus.htm

This ukulele festival in Hayward, California, is the longest-running festival on the US mainland and draws crowds each April.

www.gotaukulele.com/p/ukulele-festival-calendar_11.html

This site lists the most ukulele festivals on the planet.

Ukulele Clubs

These days you'd be hard-pressed not to find at least one ukulele group nearby. You can easily find them by a quick Internet search.

And if you don't find one? Don't fret. Years ago, I found the Vokuleles in Chico, California, through a seniors' newspaper. They had been together for more than thirty years, and I wound up leading them for their last seven. Then they reached their nineties and moved on, and the group stopped. The current ukulele craze hadn't begun yet, and we couldn't find young people who were interested in keeping it going.

My own group, the Strum Bums of Grass Valley, California, started as a class, and today performs about sixty gigs a year at convalescent, retirement, and assisted living homes, as well as schools, fundraisers, and county fairs. We have seniors and young people of all ages.

Two of my original members moved to other communities and started ukulele clubs in their new neighborhoods. One member simply approached the local YMCA and said he'd like to start a ukulele group. They were happy to give him a room and advertising support. Today that group plays gigs several times a month, is featured in festivals, and is some fifty members strong.

Bottom line is this: if you can't find a group, create one.

If you are planning a road trip across the country, bring your ukulele. Do a quick Internet search for ukulele clubs in cities where you know you will be traveling. When you sit in with a new group, play along with them, not over or under them.

Ukulele Manufacturers

The Regal Musical Instrument Company in Chicago has a history of making quality instruments for just about every manufacturer. When companies fell behind in their production needs, they farmed out their work to Regal. Harmony, Washburn, Martin, Kay, Dobro, National, and others made good use of the company. Today an old cheap Harmony ukulele with a plastic fretboard and a plywood top can sound as good as a $1,000 instrument.

Keep your eyes open for old ukuleles that can be repaired and brought back to life. Tiki King (see following list), a ukulele performer and owner of a ukulele store in Felton, California, has a huge list of ukuleles by brand. No two ukuleles sound the same, even among brands, styles, woods, and ages. They are all different.

So, let me leave you with this question and answer: How many ukuleles does a ukulele player need? Just one more. Here's a sampling of places you can find them.

www.kamakahawaii.com

Kamaka is the oldest ukulele manufacturer, founded in Honolulu more than 100 years ago.

https://kalabrand.com/pages/ukulele

Kala is a California company that has quality ukuleles made in China. The company is very active in providing inexpensive ukuleles to schools.

www.martinguitar.com/guitars/ukulele/

Martin Guitar Company made the top-of-the-line ukuleles in the 1920s and 1930s. Today, the company is once again building quality ukuleles in the US, Mexico, and elsewhere. Older Martin ukuleles are highly prized today and sought after by serious players.

www.tikiking.com/uke_database.html

Tiki King's store in Felton, California, carries a huge list of ukuleles by brand.

UKE TIP

The ukulele was the most popular instrument in the American home from 1915 to 1935. As the guitar became more and more popular, ukuleles were hidden away in closets and attics. Recently, people have been finding them and bringing them out to the light. Often they find the ukuleles are cracked from many years of temperature changes. But they are still treasures. Wood becomes more resonant when it has dried over many years, and, when rediscovered and played again, it becomes even more responsive.

Play on, Ukulalien.

INDEX

ABOUT THE AUTHOR

Dan Scanlan has been many things—an English teacher, news reporter, song-writer, software programmer, auto mechanic, layout artist, community radio personality—but the ukulele has been with him every day for more than sixty years. His songs chronicle his work experience, broken hearts, loves, humor, and sense of peace and justice. "Giant Silent Redwood," a song he composed to help save California's ancient redwoods, appeared in an English-as-a-second language textbook for middle school children. He has led several musical groups in Northern California, including Flathead, the Self-Righteous Brothers, Top Quark, Jukolin, Cool Hand Uke and the Enablers, and the Vokuleles. His current ukulele orchestra, the Strum Bums, performs some sixty gigs each year. They were featured in the *Mighty Uke* video documentary.

As the American coordinator of the 1998 project, *A Father and Son Reunion: The Braguinha Meets the Ukulele*, he returned the ukulele to its ancestral home of Madeira, Portugal. The cultural exchange resulted in a live telecast in Europe in which American and Madeiran musicians performed at the Expo '98 in Lisbon on ukulele, braguinha, and rajão. Scanlan helped create several ukulele festivals and groups and emcees the International Ukulele Ceilidh of Liverpool, Nova Scotia. A 2007 workshop in Dublin birthed Ireland's Ukuhooley club.

Scanlan has issued several cassette albums and a half-dozen CDs of original tunes, and authored the interactive ebook, *Cool Hand Uke's Way to Love Uke!* Dan has taught the ukulele for thirty years and currently has several thousand online ukulele students in seventy-two countries at Udemy.com and elsewhere. He is online at CoolHandUke.com.